POEMS and LYRICS 2021

CW00417722

INDEX

16   Christmas surprise.

17   Liverpool.

18   Shitehawk.

19   Mi wife doesn't understand me.

20   Mister media.

21   Les Tricoteuses.

22   Ruled by giant lizards from outer space (song)

23   Glad I married a witch (song)

24   Mary dear (song)

25   The seasons.

26   I love Mother Nature (song)

27   I saw a moth.

28   Me and Bob (song)

29   Fairy dust (song)

30   He crossed the bridge.

31   Childhood winters.

32   Dead Sheppey.

33   Love of our leaders (song)

34   North is going to rise again (song)

35   The English.

36   I'm not talking to you.

37   If you could know the time of your own passing.

38   Nothing's good.

39   Camping mishap #12

40   Streets of Wigan (song)

41   Xerxes scoured the sea.

42   Jayne mansfield in Howfen.

43   Gerald Seddon cawt a tench.

44   Awreet under't nazis?

45   Old boat knocking on its mooring chains.

46   Goats don't care if it's Wednesday.

47   Grave robbery.

48   I don't own a phone (song)

49   Art Awreet (song)

50   Kings of arr bommy (song)

51   Ordinary love (song)

52   Alone.

53   Owd Basher (song)

54   Romance in Ince Bar.

55   Codology.

56   I love you more than the last spoonful of custard.

57   W.H.O told the F.B.I

58   Owd woman.

59   To Jimmy.

60   Fox.

61   Everything remains the same.

62   Tiananmen square (song)

63   Corfu in France.

64   Hi Ho Mister crow.

65   At this moment (song)

66   For duck sake.

67   Peacock fancies the budgie.

68   Give us five minutes.

69   It's so easy to fall in hate (song)

70   Ferret transactions.

71   Worden park in May.

72   Marps wi thingy.

73   Phantom pongs.

74   Heid the yodelling slag heap skier (song)

75   China in my land (song)

76	God being creative.
77	Crossword fatigue.
78	Crucifix blues.
79	How "C" got over "X".
80	Glad i mowed the grass.
81	My son Pipkin.
82	The Fay.
83	Midges.
84	Car parked under Anglezarke (song)
85	A Keawyed in Paris.
86	So noble in death.
87	Sell by date.
88	Don't mention that.
89	Everything you need to know.
90	A weasel is living in the bonfire.
91	Let's make a fire and sit by it.
92	I've got a talking horse (song)
93	The first time.
94	I am man and moped.
95	All the great men (song)

96	She lived upon a rock.
97	Damn that cold east wind.
98	Average guitar player (song)
99	That Martin guitar.
100	Japanese troops on the couch.
101	Time ticking.
102	Who will cry for Angela tonight.
103	Graph of love.
104	Little star (song)
105	Kylie Minogue.
106	Birds wi nowt do.
107	Revelation on a toilet door (song)
108	Ghost bride (song)
109	Under the African moon.
110	The evening is wrong.
111	Hey you ferret face.
112	Black snow.
113	Changing things.
114	Do it like me.
115	Funfair (song)

116   Bobby (song)

117   Insignificant speck.

118   2021 resolutions.

119   Your loneliness.

120   Everyone's a singer.

121   Pass me the shotgun

122   Days of torrents (song)

123   Frond on pond (song)

124   If your teeth were made of diamonds.

125   Moaning wind (song)

126   Magic palaces.

127   Ah to be in England.

128   If there was a war (song)

129   Three storms on't trot.

130   Fading, peeling virus warnings.

131   Through a cowboy's eyes.

132   Misinformation.

133   Drizzle soup.

134   Fact checkers.

135   Painted princess of Shiffnall street (song)

136   Follow the science.

137   Let them go.

138   Beer cans in the bluebells.

139   Oscar winner's lament.

1.

Give me not your baubles nor your ladies fair,

I cannot make clear their obvious value.

Once artless was and may again I'll be,

Regaining yet the tower of the true.

Whose stark, high, arduous walls climb,

Unto a top free of fancy, fraud and foible.

If there I could just one day be,

To know myself again as nearly noble.

2.

I don't like me

Me is very bad.

Me, me, me is even worse.

In fact a little sad.

You I'm not so sure about

Her or them or it.

Existing like private planets,

In prearranged orbit.

You don't know me,

Me don't know you,

Not one little bit.

3.

Peace, love and revenge - new Country Song!

I'm going down that lonesome road to the countryside again.

I'm sick of city living, with it's heartless lying sin.

I want to wake under peaceful skies where the little birdies fly

And I'll never see another girl until the day I die.

Love and peace and understanding that will set me free.

To give me prayers to the lord above while I sit beneath the trees.

The little rabbits scuttering round the buzz of bumblebees.

And offer my forgiveness to the ones who shattered me.

But before I do I'm going to go to the city once again.

To find my girl and that bad man that caused me so much pain.

And when I do I'll take my gun and shoot him in the face.

Then forgive myself and live in peace with the whole damn human race.

4.

I awoke there with the sun, black crows were squawking.

What better time to spend than go dog walking.

My little dog is fair, she loves me cos I'm there.

How lucky on this day to be a human.

Rabbits scuttering from our path, the streams were twinkling.

Through the wet grass of the fields the fox was slinking.

My dog in beast disguise looks sweetly in my eyes

How lucky on this day to be a human

Magic moment spied a hare! its ears were twitching

Nature's green in glorious view the woods were witching

My dog she licks my face she loves me for her life.

How lucky on this day to be a human.

Far beneath fine Harrock Hill, the views were dancing.

There the sheep and little lambs in joy were prancing.

My dog she keeps me safe from all the worlds disgrace

How lucky on this day to be a human.

5.

When a sparkling acorn's shoots begins the journey of the roots

Through the ground that will support a brawny oak.

Land worked by a peasant farmer, when knights still fought in armour,

Shinny of horses, smell of woodfire smoke.

Little rootlets deeply drilling as the sapling life, God willing

Takes advantage there for it can never roam.

Through the floods and droughts and storms under the moons ivory horns,

This little patch of ground it's sacred home.

Decades come and decades go, shiny rifles usurp the bow,

In it's trunk a buried bullet marks the crime.

But this tree will not be done, leaves green reaching for the sun,

Free men soon pass, this tree is doing time.

Privileged I am to know it now to stand beneath the lofty bough,

Soon to have my own three score and ten.

The fat trunk bark is gnarled, branches, twigs, uniquely snarled,

Oblivious to the fleeting lives of men.

Future thing you will be growing when the world is overflowing

With people who never notice you are there.

My own self to console I touch your bark and sense your soul,

Feel your untamed wisdom, breathe your air.

6.

You get used to being alone, no reasons to pretend.

The biggest lie is not the one you tell to your best friend.

When there is only you, there are no games to play.

No acting or lame joking, not a single word to say.

Meditate the silence, slow the cog wheels down.

Immerse yourself in solitude, while trying not to drown.

God, I don't miss parties, always been a boring git.

Do I miss any people? Well some a little bit.

You can be alone surrounded in a city full of stink.

There is a peace not caring what other people think.

There's a tapping by the wind, soft footsteps on the stairs.

Am I really so alone, is there anybody there.

7.

I love it when the birds ride winds in arcs above the rooftops

Using its power in their playful dips and risings

Swimming and surfing the air flung out from the ponderous sea

Serious it is for them to find food and stay warm

Serious to avoid the tracking killer

Living with the wind and rain

In a daily, hard, unwritten thriller

Yet the joy of play describes the geometry of flight

Survive another day, playdream the silent night.

Evolution sparks of memory to bequeath

When men still lived in caves and birds had teeth.

8.

Tell it to my back. New song.

Never known so many experts,

Parading the moral high ground.

My ears must be burning,

From the sounds of their sounds.

And if I cant go along with it,

Maybe I deserve the birch.

Were they born so intelligent?

They must have done so much research.

Well tell it to my back, cos I don't like your front.

Maybe your motives are selfish, If I could be so blunt.

Don't wrap it up in facts.

You seived and you rinsed

Being convinced myself.

I seek not to convince.

We seem to be split,

Into two gangs these days.

And the social media,

Hosts sabre rattling affrays.

I have my own opinions,

But that's all they are.

I have nothing to say,

And I'm not a film star.

If I was an alien,

Descended from the stars.

I would look at planet earth,

Maybe then consider Mars.

Mars is uninhabitable.

And tiny in it's mass.

But one thing in common.

They are both full of gas!

9.

BERTRUM WILLIS ACTOR!!

Bertrum Willis at your service, actor!

I should have been a star you know, it's true.

I was getting to be quite big down under.

Until that business with the bloody kangaroo.

It's my agent I blame Mister Chumley

Nice chap, bats for the other side.

Well most actors do these days I think

Not a problem, thats ok, nothing to hide.

Audioned for Othello once, nearly got it.

Just fluffed a few of my lines.

But it got me a few weeks work that winter

Hupty Dumpty. St Helens, pantomime.

My problem is I'm too bloody talented

I never ever take my eye off the ball

Except one time deep in Hamlet's soliloquy

I fell arse over tit into the front stalls

I take acting ever so seriously.

Yet some audiences thinks its just fun

Laughed all the way through my Macbeth Act 3.

How was I to know my bloody flies were undone?

Leading ladies are usually my downfall.

I love evey one of them to bits.

But those revealing Victorian costumes

Can't take my eys off their armpits.

Now it's Christmas again I'm still working

And still aiming for RADA of course.

In the meantime I'm still method acting.

St Helens, back end of a bloody horse.

10.

That first Blind Date, what a farce!

Turned up with a face like a slapped arse.

Fishnet stockings, crimson lips,

Mini-skirt clinging to the hips.

Patent leather thigh high boots,

Blonde dye growing out o't roots

Black mascara, midriff bare.

And that were just me, you shoulda seen her!

11.

TRUE HOWFEN HISTORY.

It has come to the nation's realisation.

That Howfen is the cradle of civilisation.

A farmer out one morning whilst pulling up his socks,

Spied ancient hieroglyphics carved into some rocks.

Having visited the Egyptology room once at Bolton museum.

He could translate hieroglyphics as quick as he could see um.

"Thanks for the hospitality, you really quenched my thirst,

I'll name a pyramid after't Th'Horseshoe" Rameses The First.

On further investigation he found more carvings on the stone,

Evidence in Latin from the lads of Ancient Rome:

"Beltin afternoon in't Legion ended up with amnesia,

Clever drinking when pubs are closed" : Julius Caesar.

Then another note was scrawled, looked like he'd had some fun.

"We smashed Wheatsheaf to smithereens" Attilla the Hun.

"But the afternoon were ruined, in truth it made me sick,

They did what Central Asia couldn't, geet thrown out of the Vic!"

Then the farmer saw another he thought twixt Stone Age and the Iron.

Some indecipherable scramblings with a mention of White Lion.

Even further back in time another carving just said "Ugh!"

And a crude map for other cavemen to find their way to't Bug.

How Howfen has been overlooked to me it is a mystery.

I don't remember any of this when I did me "O" level history.

12.

I remember you when childish tears hung in your eyes.

Responsibility to protect you from the bitterness of life.

Then a little thing asleep with folded hands under your cheek.

Gave me a rare sense of bravery and sort of feeling weak.

Switch your lamp off quietly, the open door just might,

Let the soft light on the landing protect you through the night.

You'd ask the question "Why?", I would say "Because".

And now you are a man, stronger than I ever was.

You have growing responsibilities and mine are in decline.

You're living your future memories, maybe different than mine.

So I sit in the winter evening as the crumbling firelight dies.

I remember you when childish tears hung in your eyes.

13.

A big brother is kind and protecting

He does not make you feel afraid

He does not take away your freedom

No matter how much he is paid

He does not practice misdirection

Or use a crisis to make you miss

What he is doing with the other hand

While he gives the Judas kiss

He doesn't coax you down a friendly path

That leads by bad ways to another

That is not what big brother's do

I must be thinking of Big Brother.

14.

Back Lane East

Wringing his hands and chunnerin,

Down Back Lane East with a shuddering gait.

Is he a farmer dressed in Victorian clothes?

He's in an agitated state.

He appeared round't corner o't t'hedgerow.

Me and't dogs stood gawpin' in't wet lane.

Seemed like he didn't notice us,

Like he was on a different plane.

Wringing his hands and chunnerin,

Down the melancholy lane.

Hat and clothes, fob watch and boots,

Eyes just this side of insane.

"Good Morning", I chanced a greeting.

He passed by in silent, cold pain.

I prayed as the hair on my neck was moving

We never see that man again.

15.

As I stood on the top of the Winter Hill mast,

In a shock of visual clarity.

In that circle of sight, such a dizzying height,

I saw peace, love and human parity.

Up there all seemed well,

How could human mind tell,

The tales of a myriad blank faces.

The sadness and joys of the girls and the boys,

The pain, the rage, the disgraces.

Most of Granadaland I could see,

From the swaying pipe in the sky.

How could one perceive their hopes and beliefs

From birth till the day that they die.

Eight million souls,

Unrevealed in that view.

A precipitous, technical steeple,

Yet some manic men with a purpose and pen,

Think they understand seven billion people.

16.

A Christmas Surprise - new idea

My wife sent me to tescos This list she gave to me

Don't get anything mixed up You must read this carefully-

We need A turkey and some roasties Some baubles for the tree

Some carrots and some turnips And a nice surprise for me

Some brussels sprouts and parsnips Some nice new crusty bread

Some trifle and a Christmas pud So all will be well fed

Some sherry and some Baileys And a nice bottle of wine

And on the way back you can have a drink

If you think you have the time.

I thought I'd have the drink before

To help me on my quest To lubricate my brain cells

So i will do my best

I didn't fancy Tesco Try Lidls instead

Got Brahms and Liszt, lost the list

But I had it in my head I bought-

A vice and a welders apron

Some smokey bacon roasties

A gong, a thong and an old dipthong

A warburtons thick toastie

A pair of hiking slippers A spare wheel for the tractor

Some figs, some cigs and a Peppa Pig

And a nuclear reactor.

A bottle of Chinese vodka, a set of rosary beads

Cotton buds, Hoods, 5 pound of spuds

And a pair of jump start leads

Some rope, some dope and a climbing rope

A packet of boiled ham

Some jam, some Spam and a joint of lamb

And a picture of the pope.

When I got home twas Midnight

And my wife had gone to bed

Soon it will be Christmas and we will all be fed

I put the shopping on the table

Left Santa some mince pies

When she gets up in the morning

She'll have a wonderful surprise!

17.

So many blank preoccupied people

As we got off the resting train.

Then the city and the thick stone flags

Painted browner by the rain.

Busy morning restaurant workers

Electric scooters whizzing by.

Alien, modern, shining shop signs

Towering blocks eclipse the sky.

Bleak Victorian bulky monoliths

Built of polished Ashlar stone.

Always the same in crowded places

A unique way to feel alone.

Larger than life, The Fab Four!

Statues bolted to the ground

Looking over the rolling Mersey

A hard, grey, northern, unique sound.

18.

Here I am by the fading west

The sea is heaving and sliding.

A shitehawk shat on my Sunday best

That git deserves a good hiding.

I was hoping for inspiration

By the sea and the wind in my hat.

Write a poem to cause a sensation

But the shitehawk shat, that was that.

Creative art reduced to bits!

Just 'cos a seagull's got the shits.

19.

Mi wife doesn't understand mi

I think its cos her's from Leigh

They talk a bit funny deawn theer

Not Queen's English like thee and me.

I cawnt understand her either

I can tell there's a noise in't background

But when you're readin't sports pages

Its hard to locate ultrasound.

Nor her fault cos wimmin are different

They expect moor from a conversation

Where I can say nowt all day to nobody

They like more aural stimulation.

It all started back int thowd stone age

Cavemen were tryin't stay alive fert day

While't cavewimmin were back in cave kitchin

Plannin tactics fert next verbal affray.

While we were out slaughterin't mammoths

They were in't cave stirrin't pot

Inventin new argument phrases

While we were avoidin foot rot.

Don't get mi wrong I like wimmin

Ah look at um and I have a good laugh

Funny heaw that attractive exterior

Can hide the mind of a crazed psychopath.

20.

Mister Media.

Hello I'm Mister Media,

I'm a walking encyclopedia,

I spread my gentle brainwash,

Through the interconnected wire.

Give me scientific data,

Rows and columns, facts and figures,

And I can interpret it clearly,

In any way that you require.

What do you want them to know?

You don't have to give me reasons.

I can lie and make it become true,

I'm a con man for all seasons.

I like the constant drip feed method,

I find that works extremely well.

People can be very susceptible,

Especially when they're scared as hell.

Don't worry about the background politics,

There's a new worldwide alliance.

Just ensure you use our interpretations,

When you're following the science.

21.

Les Tricoteuses.

Oh mother dear, oh mother dear,

Please teach me how to knit.

Then on the bottom step,

Of the guillotine I'll sit.

Knitting and a'cackling,

With the revolution girls,

When they guillotine the money men,

Who control our little world.

22.

We are being ruled by Giant Lizards from Outer Space. (new song)

You're walking down the street you see a person in a hat.

You think why would anybody wear a thing like that.

It's not a fashion item, it's to control your fears,

He's wearing it to hide that fact he has no ears.

His tail curled up in his underpants its a bloody disgrace,

We're being ruled by Giant Lizards from Outer Space!

Lockdown, BLM, US elections and the rest,

Your bombarded by the news when your putting on your vest.

Wondering why the masses are running round like sheep

Still ringing in your ears when you're trying to go to sleep

Not your fault you threw that Vimto in your Mother-in-Law's face.

You're being ruled by Giant Lizards from Outer Space!

I wish I was a black actor in the adverts these days

Who's trying to educate me about the human race?

It is nothing to me really, I have no axe to grind.

But some people or things are messing around with my mind

I'm going to Hyde park corner and stand on a packing case.

"We're being ruled by Giant Lizards from Outer Space!"

Have you noticed all the newsreaders stick to the same script.

You are living in an episode of Tales from the Crypt.

Boris isn't human it is known in secret files

He's descended from Intergalactic reptiles

Totalitarian subliminal messages I can trace

We're controlled by Giant Lizards from Outer Space.

Look in the House of Commons they have slitty eyes like goats

You think that you elect them, they manipulate your votes

I was drinking in the pub, there was a bloke, don't get me wrong

He was licking out his bitter with a long forked tongue

I'm building my own rocket, Uranus my preferred place.

We're being ruled by Giant Lizards from Outer Space.

23.

New song - Glad I Married a Witch.

I was a drinker, I was a stinker,

Had I been a woman I'd have been a bitch.

On a downward ramp to become a tramp

Then I married a witch.

She stopped me drinking, she stopped my stinking,

She could tidy the house with a flick of her wrist.

To get me in motion she made me a potion

Glad I married the witch.

She made three children in her cauldron,

Witchette, Bobby and Dippy-Doo

From puppy dogs tails and three pints of ale

Funny with magic what you can do.

We had no money so she strangled a bunny

Then turned it into a bundle of cash.

We had no house so she took off her blouse

One erected in a blinding flash.

Then she got bolder with a crow on her shoulder

She turned it into a chateau in France

With vineyards and lakes to drown her mistakes

Around the garden we dance.

At the end of October providing she stays sober.

She hosts a party for the children of the damned.

We dance round the fire in suitable attire.

Me and the hunchback of Notre Dame.

Now the bad days are banished and the children have vanished

We live in isolation surrounded by a ditch.

To keep me vital she smothers me in trifle

Glad I married a witch.

24.

New song - Mary Dear.

Mary dear, I sense you near,

Though you're gone four hundred year.

In this place, in this hall,

Living death in every wall

I see your portrait, young and fair

The dusk light agitates your hair

Up the stairs to bed I creep

I feel you breathing while I sleep

The morn is misted o're the lake

When my little walk I take

Among the pebbles harsh and bare

I see it softly shining there

Your gold ring, your lost gold ring

Given in secret from your king

Your only token of his love

Forbidden by the Lord above

When it was lost the sad tale says

You could not live more barren days

I found your tomb, your sepulchre

I slid the lid and said a prayer

I placed it gently that gold band

The finger of your skeletal hand

A soft wind blew my fear away

I walked in sunlight on that day.

I spend my evening solitaire

No soft footsteps on my stair

No soft breathing in my bed

I wish sometimes you were still undead.

25.

THE SEASONS (A brief explanation)

In olden times there was just one titled season.

Winter was the only period with a name.

Prepare for its hard coming was the reason.

The rest of the year was more or less the same.

Then some smart arse invented the word Summer,

To denote anti-winter as an entity.

Then someone thought about the time between the two.

Let's give those ups and down their own identity.

As plants sprung from the ground they called that Spring.

Then called it Harvest when the food was ripe.

The word Autumn was invented in 1300.

By a bloke outside a pub smoking a pipe.

Fall was English too as poetic expression.

When leaves fall the word describes it well.

And this was then picked up by the Americans.

Because it is the easiest one to spell.

26.

I love mother nature

And I like being on my own

You can't call me later

Cos I don't own a phone

You can't ring me, you can't ping me,

You can't trace my location

Being out of the swell of the modern world,

That is my vocation.

You can't pace me, you can't trace me,

You can't put me in your data groups,

You can't rate me or certificate me,

Cos I won't jump through your hoops.

You can't update me or berate me,

Cos I'm outside the scope of your control

Throw your phones in the sea and come with me

Walk straight through their black hole.

I don't need to buy an upgrade

Or download the newest app,

You can't upgrade what you don't have

In the first place my dear chap.

You can't bell me, you can't tell me,

What you think that I should do.

Silent and free sitting in this tree

I don't think I'll miss the phones or you.

27.

I saw a moth pretending to be a leaf.

Or was it a leaf pretending to be a moth?

Sweet droplet of rain holding,

Before gravity makes it plop.

More trees than ever on Mother Earth

Incessant life eternal springing

Coping with the freaky humans

Show them beauty, keep them singing

Doctor Death plans domination

From his steel, electric tower!

Oh the sensory bliss of sunlight

Illuminating a fragile flower.

28.

New Song - Me and Bob.

The rain was hard in 63, when we met the wind was blowin.

When I heard that tambourine I knew, I'd follow where it was going

When I first saw that Highway, I was a thin man all alone.

But I liked that cool isolation, made me feel like a rolling stone.

All my friends they disliked you, that made me like you more.

My love she spoke like silence in the shade of heaven's door.

In 69 in an English field with 200,000 more.

When you walked on the stage in that white suit 200,000 roared.

Funny for a lad who bummed around and sang for drinks and tips.

To be standing there without a care with the world at your fingertips

When I went home and went back to school, I wanted to be like you.

How was I to know back then, I had to join the back of the queue.

Now life has passed and times have changed and I feel I'm growing old

I will never forget the spark you lit that made me feel so bold.

And as I read by candle light dusty books from off the shelf.

What a gift you gave from womb to grave, to reason for yourself.

Now music comes and music goes, some wonderful some din.

But I still walk behind your Spanish boots when my ship comes rollin' in.

29.

New Song. Where is the fairy dust?

I was feeling sorry for myself

So I hit myself in the face with a wet kipper

Metaphorically speaking of course

But I've been this way since I was a nipper.

Where are the happy pills

Where is the fairy dust

Sprinkle ecstasy around your life

Wake up in the morning in a ditch of disgust.

Some comedians have brilliant gifts

But in silent rooms they turn off their light

Woman donkey stoning her front step

Makes a statement that her world is all white

Ever see a kitten with a gloomy mood

Or an awkward tree that won't take sunlight

I used to know a woman with a smiley face

From her waking breath till she conked out at night.

Maybe there's a lesson to be learned from this

But I'm not quite sure I'll check my briefcase

Maybe good to stay away from happy pills

Keep a kipper close to slap your daft face.

30.

He crossed the bridge and he burned it.

Confident of his foreseen fate.

Funny how things that seemed so ordinary,

On looking back seem so great.

31.

I remember winter's when't snow were twice as tall as me

An we had to walk down dug eawt corridors wi freezin feet

An the slides we made in't playground from one end to the other

Come whom wi blue hands, cuts and bruises to show off to me mother

Ice on't mornin windows as we looked out wi smokin breath

I liked it too when't smog came deawn an choked us half to death

It were beltin that smog it tasted like summat eawt of hell

An you couldn't even see your feet, we walked by sense of smell

But I thowt it were good for a change, like livin on't planet Mars

Wi ghostly headlights on't th'A6 flying saucers made from cars

Funny on a day like this when't burnin' sun is crackin't flags

Hard to imagine days like that tryin't feel warmth from lightin fags.

32.

Poor dead sheppey lying in't road

Neck bent at a tragic angle

Killed by a flying car I think

Left in a tarmac mangle

I'll pick thee up by a worthless wing

Don't want thee squashed no more

When magic light shone in them eyes

As through the sky you'd soar

And with your pals when time was right

With telepathic co-operations

You'd dance your geometric delights

In impossible murmurations.

33.

The Amazing Love of our Leaders. (new words)

Boris Johnson and Tony Blair

These are the ones who really care

I bet they can't get to sleep at night

Instructing us plebs about wrong and right.

Oh that we could be like them

Justin Trudeau and Joe Biden

Look and listen there's so much to learn

From the pious face of Jacinda Ardern

Amazing love our leaders gave

To teach stupid people how to behave

Amazing love how can it be

That these great men should care for me.

How could it be that I refuse

To sit and watch the BBC news

Without their dose of moral guidance

I might resort to drink and violence.

New laws they pass, they do their best.

Not with one ounce of self interest.

Modern day saints so brave and true.

The elite really know what's best for you.

A struggling mother with her life in bits.

Really needs advice from spoilt Notting Hill gits.

Living off a pittance and on the skids.

They'll tell her whats best for her kids.

They nurture us put food on our shelves,

They never worry about themselves.

When the virus is over then God forbid,

They'll all stand proud say "Look what we did!"

34.

New Song - The North is going to rise again.

The flag is hanging flat against the pole,

Black Poplar leaves are slowly turning brown,

I saw the key floating on the water,

Reached out to get it and caused it to go down.

Just do a little bit of work each blessed day,

When it's finished you can rest and you'll be fain.

And when't smokes twirling up the chimney,

Dream the North is going to rise again.

Rise again, rise, rise again,

From the fallen factory chimneys,

Rucks steaming in the pouring rain,

Put your hand inside my hand,

Put your hand inside my cold hand.

The mills are rotting in the wind,

Bones of miners groaning under the ground,

New shopping centres clean and sparkling,

Shops boarded up in the middle of the town.

Everything changes and sometimes I think,

Maybe those soldiers died for nothing then.

But some old glory still remains in our hearts,

And the North is going to rise again.

35.

I worked for a fortnight in Dumfries

The people were mostly nice.

They didn't much like the English,

But I was only threatened twice.

Then they sent me down to Cardiff

Where there's a welcome in the valleys

For people of all nations

Except for the English scallys.

I think they liked me in Ireland,

Kept saying "Ain't he a one!"

But I'm sure when I walked out the pub,

I could hear "Thank God he's gone"

Now here in South West France,

English are all over the place.

And to be brutally honest about it,

Some are a bloody disgrace.

Haughty, loud and pushy,

From cafe to supermarket shelf.

I hate the bloody English

I'm a racist to myself!

36.

I'm not talking to you

Cos you don't agree with me.

Well I'm not talking to you!

Just you wait and see.

When half the world won't talk,

We'll have to live in shifts,

And on our way to life,

We'll have to use these lifts.

You know that woman across the road,

She doesn't think the same,

As the rest of us on this street,

Now we know who to blame.

I am so obviously right

How can you not see?

You are incredibly stupid

If you don't agree with me.

37.

If you could know the time of your own passing,

How would you spend your life from now till then.

Different from our current daily wasting,

Such is the common fate of all just men.

Some are so hard working, never resting,

When'ere their toil is noble or just grind.

Not keen to dwell on philosophic questions,

Too tired to fill that vacancy of mind.

To put your fears at rest I'll solve the problem.

Take note dear reader this answer's just for you,

Get the ale in, enjoy every sandwich.

You kick the bucket next Tuesday, half past two.

38.

When nothing's good, nothing's good

No matter how you wrap it up

No matter how you try till a tear burns in your eye

And you pour some dry vodka in your cup

Nothing's good

When the circle of life arrives at

The time when nothing's good

Doesn't matter how you try appreciation

Too late, cos fate won't let you appreciate

The desert from the flood

When nothing's good.

When nothing's good you can't make

A sod into a cake, you can't take Satan's horns

Make him a saint.

Because he is what he is and that's show biz

And you can't be something good when you ain't.

39.

Camping Mishap #12

I was yawning in the awning

The tent was bent

Grass was wet and luscious

And I hadn't got a cent

The cook was in the brook

Catching fishes for the dishes

I remembered then the embers

Light the fire, a bit ambitious

I blew and blew and blew and it grew

From the cinder to the tinder grass

Games of flames frames James

Turnaround and warm my ass

Fire going, blowing, blowing

Cook screams Got one!, and its a hot one

Fires nearly ready flames are burning steady

Ran to the van get a pan for the plan

Heat the water for the slaughter

Toiling broiling water's boiling

Bring the pan! Bring the pan!

Throw the fish in if you can

Running cross the wet grass with a pan of boiling water

Past the line of waking campers and the mother and the daughter

Pointing giggling laughing at the creature from the awning

Running cross the Keswick campsite bollock naked in the morning.

40.

Gutters cracked and leaking rain

Like I'm living in a story again

Not sure where I'm going to be tonight

There's a lost dog on the street

On a corner where the people meet

Looking for peace when everything wants to fight

Scent of a chippy in the air but its no good for me

I'll be eating wind and rain and silence for my tea

Unless I, Get the old cracked guitar out

Find a doorway where the owner won't shout

Sing a few songs with the people passing by

They're rushing and pushing and on the phone

Feel like I'm stood here all alone

My hats in the rain but my head is keeping dry

Oh there, a lady fair, and a present for me

Gleaming brightly in my hat the wondrous fifty P!

Just need a few more like that

fives, tens, twenties in my hat

Who knows the odd noble golden pound

Then maybe god will stop this rain

We can look for that old chippy again

Me and the lost dog may again be found.

Well it may be a story for me

For some this is reality

Each moment hoping for the good ones to give

Just a little bit the odd spare change

I know you're embarrassed I look so strange

This is who I am and this is where I live.

God bless the homeless ones when autumn's on the breeze

Not all in far off lands on these streets and on their knees.

41.

Xerxes scourged the sea at Hellespont

When a storm washed his bridges away

He gave the raging waves three hundred lashes

That will teach the storms and seas to obey

The mighty Xerxes then sent his blacksmiths down

With glowing irons to brand the naughty sea

Demanding in a fit of human pride

Look at me feeble nature, take the knee!

It seems our brand new world has modern Xerxes'

World leaders lashing seas with their mind

Each one trying to out Xerxes the other

Look at me, the saviour of mankind!

42.

Jayne Mansfield, Hollywood to Howfen.

I saw her walkin down them steps after bouncer opened't door.

I fell in love, I were 14 and she were 34.

Long shiny dress, pure blonde hair, little dogs in her arms,

Big fur coat and high heeled shoes, we'd just come from't farm.

Me and Kevin Purtill stood in't rain for th'Hollywood superstar

Little did we know a few weeks later she'd be killed in her car

This owd bloke shouted "Ee love they't bonny", across the Howfen night.

She smiled and said "Gee thanks", never seen teeth so white.

When I read about her death I thowt whatever browt thee theer

Stood on th'Empire steps in Howfen, and I shed a little tear.

43.

Gerald Seddon cawt a tench at Rat Pit

He were on is own it broke top length in two

Me and Clucker were poncin abeawt at Cromptons

Tryin't catch four ounce carp, we'd geet a few

Seddy come sheawtin over fields to us

He were mobilised dancin a frantic jig

Ah didn't know what he were gooin on abeawt

Till a heard him cry "Yo call them buggers big!"

Thowd tench were very slimy an he missed it

So we follered him back to't scene of his crime

Believin, misbelievin size o't monster

So we thowt wid adjudicate his catch this time

Sure enuf again he hooked that Tinca Tinca

And doubtin him a felt like such a plonker

He pulled it in and theer it were pantin on it side

No doubtin neaw to us that were a chonker

We kissed it, stroked it, unhooked its lip

Made sure it were awreet and free to go

Seddy taught me some philosophy that mornin

Don't doubt too much because you never really know.

44.

It would have been awreet under't Nazis

As long as you didn't step out of line

Show respect, follow the rules

You stupid Englisch Schwein!

Fantastic roads and factories

He were clever that Hitler bloke

Don't mention those camps in the woods

Ignore that funny smelling smoke

Enjoy your life of freedom

Behind your brand new sparkling fence

Your leaders know what's best for you

Obey them, it makes sense.

45.

Old boat knocking on its mooring chains

Rocking by the rotting harbour wall

Salt scent breeze singing off the sea

Sunset sad as dipping seagulls call

Tide foam sand and seaweed

Washing tick-tocking on the rocks

People pass in pairs, curving promenade

Pub lights turning on the human clocks

Ship on the horizon, storm coming in

My back is cold against the iron pier

Funny how you see things differently

When new days come and old days disappear.

46.

Goats don't care if it's Wednesday

Cats don't go preying in church

Budgie's won't contemplate suicide

Though they've wasted their life on a perch

Owls aren't impressed by your trainers

No matter which make you have bought

Hedgehogs don't give money to charity

Even though some of them think that they ought

Great white sharks are not fussy eaters

Gordon Ramsey could be on their menu

Dogs aren't self conscious about sex

They just do it regardless of venue

Mice don't get drunk every weekend

Well some do who live in pub cellars

But they don't beat their wives or repeat rubbish jokes

Like rats and some human fellers

Seagulls can be messy eaters

But they don't fill the sea with their plastic

And ducks never start a world war

Just the odd fight, nothing too drastic

Badgers aren't hot on philosophy

Most weasels don't push modern art

And my Lottie can't understand love and romance

But there's something there deep in her heart.

47.

True story with a few lies.

When I were young I had to go wi mi mother to't thowd churchyard.

I didn't know why we were going but I hadn'nt got a choice

She were talkin to an owd woman and I were stood theer waitin

When the wind blew mi eyes to look around the sound of a whisprin voice

Theer behind me a monolith o granite graveyard stone

A family tomb with a little wall built in a ten foot square

Inscribed wi words I couldn't read because I couldn't read

And theer filled in wi diamond white stones, could I, would I dare.

She couldn't see me bendin down pretentin't tie me shoe

So I pinched two o them jewels and put em in me hankie

That neet when it were time for bed I took me treasure out

Admired their glistening nowtiness I were feelin very swanky

I lifted me pillow and placed um theer, a happy smilin thief

But in the night such an awful thing, a fricknin thing a spies

A little mon come crawlin out from the bottom o me bed

He were black and smelt rotten, two white grave stones for his eyes

The followin day I took them stones an a run cross Manchester road

I geet to't grave and a put em back and said a little prayer

I'm sorry God a took these stones an ahl never do it again

Made't sign o't cross and run back wom regrettin me nowty dare

When't wind turns black and rain boils deawn and night's as nowt as nast

Rememember cover't mirrors whenever there's a storm

Don't pinch things from graveyards, alus check under't bed

And keep thi socks on under't covers, soft and safe and warm.

48.

New Song - I don't own a phone!

I love mother nature

And I like being on my own

You can't call me later

Cos I don't own a phone

You can't ring me, you can't ping me,

You can't trace my location

Being out of the swell of the modern world,

That is my vocation.

You can't pace me, you can't trace me,

You can't put me in your data groups,

You can't rate me or certificate me,

Cos I won't jump through your hoops.

You can't update me or berate me,

Cos I'm ouside the scope of your control

Throw your phones in the sea and come with me

Walk straight through their black hole.

I don't need to buy an upgrade

Or download the newest app,

You can't upgrade what you don't have

In the first place my dear chap.

You can't bell me, you can't tell me,

What you think that I should do.

Silent and free sitting in this tree

I don't think I'll miss the phones or you.

49.

The moon is waxing gibbous this evening.

It's saying "Come on lad its time to make a change"

But changing, really changing, that's a bugger.

Like reaching out for something out of range.

Art awreet? Ahm awreet whtever awreet means etc.

See I cawnt believe a thing I hear on't telly.

Read in't papers, social media's chattering beaks.

Sometimes I think I'm living in a story.

Conspiracy theory? Aye lad give it a few weeks.

Who is going't come out of this the better

I bet it won't be th'ordinary man in't street.

Look after thisel, Look after all your loved ones.

Say your prayers under't waxing moon toneet.

50.

The Kings of Arr Bommy. (New song written today on Bastille day in France)

I'm a soldier, I'm a sentry, I'm on duty.

I've got a big stick and a peagun, its a beauty.

If any of them marauders come up Church street,

We'll fight them, we'll defend it, we're all armed to't teeth.

Arr Bommy is the best Bommy round here.

Made of planks, boxes, trees and an owd cheer.

Its four hundred foot tall and half a mile wide

And there's room fer all't gang, secret den on th'inside.

Nobody will dismantle arr Bommy.

Not a Nazi or a Leyther or a Commie

Me and me brother and Charlie and Tommy

We're the kings, we're the kings of arr Bommy.

I've geet bangers and I'll use them if I must.

They'll turn them pesky varmints to dust.

Alan Shields says he's even geet a rocket

And ahve getten six good skimmers in me pocket.

Me tommy guns geet telescopic seets

I can murder things from a million feet.

I can shoot um in't middle o't neet.

Cos it's got leets and three feet.

Even't wenches in our gang con feyt.

Thingy's sister's dead tall stood up straight

If she has a wash we con use her to charm um

Then we'll cut em off at pass and disarm em.

I think yon mon's a Japanese spy

He keeps askin abeawt Bommy, how high?

I ses its nowt do wi thee, but its plain tha con see.

Arr Bommy goes reyt up to the sky.

51.

Ordinary Love. (New little song)

She had ice blue sparking eyes, she was a little overweight,

Her laugh could twinklify the room, her teeth weren't geometric straight,

She'd never hurt a living thing, she was almost always late,

She didn't sneer or turn him down when he asked her on the date

She was perfect.

He didn't look like that Brad Pitt and he worked on building sites,

He liked a few pints with his pals but he'd never start a fight,

When she spoke he tried to listen, but he didn't always get it,

But he was soft with her kitten, when it bit him he would let it,

He was perfect.

The night was cold, the night was dark,it started drizzling in the town,

His car kept stalling and spluttering, the cafe looked a bit run down,

But the fire was burning bright and the food was cheap and good.

Their chatter silly, embarrassing, first awkward kiss blazed his blood.

It was perfect.

52.

The shock,the torment, the future looms bleak

My brain writhing and snapping, the mind of a freak

Of nature evolving but the direction is weak

More different two seconds ago than last week

I don't want to listen, the words people speak

Pulling and picking your soul with their beak

A mass of unchangeable steel, stone and teak

What am I then? a spark of nothing unique

The din of humanity the visions that reek

Of death and obscenity, yet some angels still seek

The answers that calm the fears of the meek

I can't hold on to that goodness the messages leak

So I sit on the step with the dogs of an evening

When the warmth of the sun still is haunting the stone

And I stroke them, talk to them in words and they listen

And I then realise we're all completely alone.

53.

I can beat thee at anythin bar feeytin!

I said to owd Basher in't pub.

He said, reet I'll play thi at dominoes,

Then we'll hit snooker tables at t'club.

I whupped him at both of them disciplines.

Then round t'board at darts I did fine,

I'd finished ont double and th'inner,

While he were still aiming fert nine.

Then we joined in the quiz and I won it,

Coming last he sat theer like a vulture.

But a lifetime of boozing and feeytin,

Don't prepare you for Art, Science and Culture.

Then I said ahl race thi to't Lion.

I beat him wi seconds to spare.

They'll have to get th'ale in now Basher,

And he did with never a care.

"So theay beat me at everything Jimmy"

"It's been a grand neet, thanks a bunch"

So I stood up fert shake th'hand o't good loser,

He knocked me out with only one punch.

54.

Romance in Ince Bar.

My girlfriend came from Ince.

Eyes of cobalt sunset rinse.

With a figure that could rival that Jayne Mansfield.

She'd got a sister just as fit,

But I think she had to flit,

And got a flat in Ashton-in-Makerfield.

I apologise for that last rhyme,

But if you have a little time,

I would like to tell you more about my stunner.

We met in old Ince Bar,

So she hadn't travelled far,

And was available cos her husband did a runner.

Loving her was not some duty,

She had a heart deep natural beauty,

With a sparkle that could set your spirit free.

I couldn't cope, I wasn't thinking.

I was doing too much drinking.

Then the drink, you know, it started drinking me.

Tomorrow is another day.

What's it matter anyway.

I told myself to counteract the pain.

Freedom quells your fears,

And no-one can see your tears,

When you're walking home through Hindley in the rain.

55.

CODOLOGY

I didn't pay much attention at school,

I was hopeless at Maths and Biology.

Well I don't brag normally and it wasn't awarded formally,

But I've got an honours degree in Codology.

To excel in codolology and bullshitterology,

You need to be very hard faced.

If you're caught out lying at least you were trying,

And for that there is no disgrace.

This degree is a must to maintain your distrust

Of leaders and media who sell,

New types of morality, accept change as normality,

Cos they're probably lying as well.

If you don't feel easy with the new ways of thinking

Don't feel isolated and blue.

Retain a strong doubt when elite ones speak out.

See, they're usually bullshitting too.

We've been ambushed and fooled by the good guys who rule,

Retake your codology qualifications.

Add to this a dynamic gob and you might get a job,

With the Government or United Nations.

56.

I love you more than the last spoonful of custard

From my Mother's Christmas sherry trifle.

More than when a politician appears just when I'm polishing

The telescopic lens of my expensive vintage Italian rifle.

I love you more than a little kitten's face,

As it looks up dripping from a bowl of creamy milk,

Or the opening bars of Like a Rolling Stone

Or wind dried sheets when they feel like silk.

I love you more than when I found that lost tenner

Screwed up in the pocket of my pants,

Or the way some women roll their rrrr's

When they are talking to me in France.

Or the the sun shining through a broken window pane

Makes a prism rainbow light the dust.

More than a wrought iron gate clanging shut dead straight

Shedding bits of 200 year old rust.

I love you more than when I threw my company phone

In the Leeds Liverpool canal with relief.

Or when me and Dave and Big Dave drove like mad

Then jumped out and got that scumbag thief.

I love you more than the rage of hundred mile winds

Blowing through the top of the Winter Hill mast

And the days of calm and the days of peace,

And the days of love that can never last.

57.

W.H.O told the FBI ten million people are going to die.

Then Maccy D tried to arrange to blame KFC for climate-chnge.

DWP told the BBC that the NHS is on its knees.

B and Q and C and A say the QVC sales end today.

The CEO with a URL told the FAQs to go to hell.

NASA sacked their CSOs cos they started beliving in UFOs.

WWF and RSPCA dont accept gifts from YMCA.

 PRC say we'll sell you free plastic crap stay on your knees.

NATO told the old EU we're leaving what you gonna do.

HSBC told the IRM that the UPS delivers SPAM.

Then UPS said that GPO are the Royal Mail if you didn't know.

A BBW with a low IQ joined a dating site called the Human Zoo.

AT the EOD the ETA will be OTT in a shortened way.

LGBT and the Q may run out of letters soon.

RSPCA couldn't say if they sold fur coats through C and A.

BLM say to KKK supremacists have had their day.

INTERPOL told the Daily Mail NSPCC is going to fail.

ITV said to Channel 4 that HR is a revolving door.

The CCB told the RFU sweet FA we try too.

Slow down MRS hit the brakes, everybody makes mistakes.

DHSS, FBI, DEA, CSI,

Marks and Spencer, B and Q

NGO's Chester Zoo

NI declare UDI

Outsiders can't fathom why

Your DOB? have HIV? Let me know RSVP.

58.

Owd woman bending down on her knees

Her front step wanted donkey stoning.

A mother hangin her wet washin out,

Under grey clouds slow and groanin.

Some lads jumped off red 16 bus

Glum conductor dinged his bell.

A few cars passing along th'A6,

Spluttering motorbike as well.

Scent o't chippy firing up,

Owd mon wi a bucket of coal.

Mrs Thingy lookin through't curtains,

Th'owd mon puts wood in th'ole.

Robert Hartley had done a good drawing,

Of a woman wi no clothes on.

He said dunt her favver glamorous

I thowt her just looked daft and frozen.

I pinched a bottle o warm milk,

Off a step, there were nobody in.

I glugged it all an it tasted good,

Even though I knew it were a sin.

There were a cowboy on at th'Empire

Bur I didn't have any money.

Saturday mornin top o Church street

Everything seemed a little bit funny.

59.

To Jimmy.

Farewell old friend

When I was up against it you were there.

When it was me against the gangs, you didn't scare,

You were always there.

The good things about living, the walks and the chats,

Nature and mountains, laughing and working,

You were always so good at that.

Now I've lost a friend who is irreplaceable.

Your wisdom and your strength, your smiling face.

Today this world is less interesting.

Today this world is a lonelier place.

60.

I woke this morning and I'd grown a long bushy tail just like a fox.

I was scared of going out and getting ridiculed.

I tucked it up behind my shirt and went shopping.

But nobody in the supermarket was fooled.

Giggling, pointing talking behind their hands,

My bushy tail stuck out like a sore thumb.

Then an old lady walked past the vegetables aisle,

With a bushy tail growing out above her bum.

So they all started pointing, laughed at her for a bit,

She looked so silly I almost joined in.

Then I realised what am I laughing at her for,

Me and her are of the same bushy tail kin.

Maybe when I go out shopping tomorrow.

Most people will have long bushy tails.

We can all laugh at the ones who haven't got one yet.

Being in the majority, it never fails.

61.

There'll be cold snow blowing somewhere today

Under this unforgiving star.

Is the dust at the side of this old road

The same as the dust in old Zanzibar.

No matter where you wake and find yourself,

No matter where your soul longs to roam,

The drink and the drugs and the old mood swings,

They pack a case and go wherever you go.

Here they are driving on the wrong side of the road,

And they don't seem to care for tea.

Well I can hardly understand a thing they say,

And I think they feel the same about me.

Some groups of people want me to agree with them,

I can never understand the reasons why.

The only things we will ever have in common,

Is being born and then we all have to die.

So when the spinning sun in the west declines

And old church bells ring out its flame

I will still be here but on a different road.

But everything remains the same.

You can duck and dive and drink and cry,

You can find another person to blame.

You can look in the mirror or dig yourself a burrow,

But everything remains the same.

62.

New song - The lad in Tiananmen Square

You've heard about the miner's strikes and the charge of the Light Brigade.

When you're up against the odds and try hard not to be afraid.

Stand up for what you believe in, on your own if you really dare,

Then think about that lad in Tiananmen Square,

He didn't get a medal or a meeting with the queen,

Where he comes from it's black and white with nothing in between.

Braver than 300 Spartans, outranking all that dare.

The man who stood in front of the tanks in Tiananmen Square.

We've all gone soft in the west, luxuries we don't need um.

Got used to living lazy, take for granted what is freedom.

Well watch your back and think on, this sort of living's really rare.

Think about that lad in Tiananmen Square.

What's his name and where's his history, where's the blue plaque on the wall

Where the gravestone if he's dead or did they give him one at all.

When your feeling violated and when no-one seems to care.

Think about that lad in Tiananmen Square.

The whole wide world was watching and the anger was profound.

But a few days later in that square there was nobody around.

We all got on with normal life and politicans they made friends.

With the tyrants and the murderers that's how the story ends.

And you buy cheap goods just like I do, toys and picnic tables,

There always seems to be that same old name on the labels.

And the money men get richer and the media toe the line.

To all intents and purposes everything is bloody fine.

But in a quiet moment when all seems peaceful everywhere.

Think about that lad in Tiananmen Square.

63.

There's a Corfu on here in France

You haft be in thouse for nine

That's eight o clock in Lancashire

No, in Germany that's nein.

I'm a continental sort of lad

I can talk shite in several tongues

Nowt new theer though

I'm misunderstood in Tyldesley Bongs

Planes are all parked up rusting

Don't think I'll ever be coming back

Feels like stuck in dead end street

What's french for cul-de-sac?

64.

Hi Ho Mister crow

You always know which way to go

Flapping high or skulking low

Black heart savage thing

Pecking, cawing, swooping, ripping

Flesh of taken young blood dripping

See a man! Caw, Caw, you chicken.

Stay away from him.

How do you know you bullying thing?

Taker, slicer, savage King

Time to stride on oil black wing.

You know to stay away from him.

65.

Enjoy the moment.

When you're walking home from work on a Thursday evening in November.

And the pub lights coming on and the jukebox countdown thud,

Of the bass guitar beginning of Waterloo Sunset.

You've got money in your pocket, you're not ill, and all is good.

Hello moment, special moment,

I like your singularity.

At this moment, what is lacking?

Nothing when you are free.

When the cat curls on the couch and the little dogs are sleeping,

By the fire gradely burning, softly glowing in the grate.

When the western wind is whistling in the wires on the pylons,

And the gentleness of evening takes your coat and seals your fate.

When the past is finally silent and the future doesn't matter.

And you know your not important, not in charge, you never were,

Just a cluster of atoms beneath the silent moon ascending,

 Lucky to be lucky, for that moment to be there.

And a little voice is wandering in the old streets of your memory,

Reminds you of the back yards and the football and the friends.

Each little spec of memory warms a corner of your cosmos,

This moment is forever, a moment never ends.

66.

For Duck Sake.

All the birdies in the sky look at us and wonder why.

Peace doves rest from all their cooing, Just what are those humans doing?

Geese and goslings, duck and drake think of us say Duck sake!

Little flies and beetles too wonder what we're trying to do.

Three toed sloth almost delirious waking thinks "You cannot be serious"

The might Ash the might Oak sense us near and share a joke

If you're so clever thinks the squid, clever is as clever did.

"Numb as piss stones" says the ant, "I concur" says the elephant.

Hyena laughed and laughed, what's so funny, he thinks we're daft.

The combined intelligence of the worms realise we can't beat germs.

On her eggs the ostrich sits, refers to us as stupid gits.

Even budgies can do the maths, we're the only race of psychopaths.

Building, breeding, cutting down, change Nirvana to a town.

Models on the catwalks prance, babies starving while we dance.

Even the most useless slugs don't get addicted to hard drugs.

Meanwhile in the evening sky the little birdies say bye bye.

67.

The peacock is fancying the budgie.

The fireash is finished and cold.

The weeds are magnificently greening.

The buds and the blossoms unrolled.

The logs are asleep for the Summer.

The hill woods a magical feel.

Blue sky is shrinking the clouds away.

And the sunset colours unreal.

Pondlife is twitching and wriggling.

Life is a beautiful thing.

It's late, missed the boat, didn't bring a note.

But it feels like the first day of Spring.

68.

Give us five minutes and I'll sort it out.

I'll sort it out if I can.

Things get heavy, they can get too much.

It's the pain of being a man.

Things are expected, responsibilities,

I'll put kettle on, we'll have a brew.

Weren't that long ago when we were kids,

We'd laugh at world me and you.

You're supposed to be strong, supposed to be brave,

Supposed to be sure with no doubt.

But life gets bleak and and days get dark,

And you can't see any way out.

We'll sort it out, don't you worry,

After a brew we can go for a walk.

I've got ears and I can listen,

Even grown men can have a proper talk.

When they're coming at you from every side,

Too much on your own to face.

Don't worry owd lad, tell me what's up.

You're here, you're in the right place.

69.

Its so easy to fall in hate

Especially when you don't feel too great

When your self love is in danger

Always better to blame a stranger

Its so easy/my loss your albatross

It's so easy to be a lazy thinker

Especially when the question is a stinker

When your life's left on the shelf

Take it out on someone else

Its so easy/my inability your liability

When your heart has felt a pang

Go and join a hateful gang

Your life is stretched by ropes and pulleys

Don't deal with it just join the bullies.

Its so easy/my silence their violence

70.

Ferret transactions.

Wheer art'a gooin wi yon ferret?

Ahm tekin it t'be put sleep.

Heaw owd is it, nice little feller,

It were two on Tuesday last week.

Ahl gi thi one an eight fer that ferret,

Mek it two bob the ferret is thine,

Cum here little beauty to daddy,

It bit mi! nowty little swine.

Ahm bleedin neaw, look at mi finger,

Look what thi ferret just did.

Its tha ferret now thea just bowt it,

Why'st think I were tryin' get rid.

Gi it back and ahl gi thee a shillin,

A shillin!, Ah gi thee two bob

Ah bur its damaged goods neaw theys nine moor fingers,

It'll probably finish the job.

Awreet gi us a bloody shillin,

Tek nowty bugger, it gi me a freet.

Come on gnasher, lets find't next sucker

We're havin a lucrative neet!

71.

Worden park in May.

Nothing quite so melancholy as a rainy English park.

When a cold wind out of nowhere blasts the sheets of cloud to dark.

Unfolding macs, umbrellas and running for some shelter

As the slides become unslideable as a one way helter-skelter

The swings are swinging on their own as the sand pit turns to mush

Then the hail in slapping sheets turn the puddles into slush.

The teenage girls with glossy lips, clothes and trainers crazy cost

Huddled waiting near the Ladies seeking things already lost.

Then the May sun comes a-blastin as it's capable of doing.

And the car park goes to steaming like a tarmac tea's a brewing.

Graceful lonely trees cry artistic tears upon the lawn

The park becomes a painting when the people have all gone.

72.

I were playin a game o marps wi thingy from near't th'Horshoe.

Awlus thowt it were a stupid game but it were't th'outer limits o thingy's IQ.

Threw mi glass sphere into't dust while considering pain free suicide.

Then I geet a release as mi mother cawd mi't come in for mi tea inside.

Next day I had't go't t'church and listen to um chantin in Latin.

Sat next to this owd woman singin, Ah thowt I wish someone ud let cat in.

Next day sat in't classroom ah thowt this is wastin' time sunshine stealin'

And then playin marps wi daft thingy suddenly became more appealin'

73.

Phantom pongs!

Cleaning the house with a magic wand and a fag.

A Brillo pad a scraper and a brush.

I'm looking for the origin of a funny pong

No it's not me before you say it mush!

It smells like rotten eggs with a hint of vanilla

I smelt it once in a market in Algiers

I open all the doors and Dettol all the floors

The following day it magically reappears.

I looked behind the fridge for a dead mouse or a bird.

The things that cats leave us for a present.

No nothing there, or underneath the stair

It's here again and getting more unpleasant.

Do ghosts have a scent that follows them around?

Does a tree emit a cry when you fell it.

Does the lonely tree fall without a sound?

An odour in an empty room? Can you smell it?

It wasn't in this room, then it was.

Maybe ghost smells can pass straight through a wall.

Or is my imagination running riot.

Maybe it is just me after all.

74.

Heidi the yodelling slag heap skier.

She sits on 't slag heap on a Sunday morn

Doesn't matter if its raining, if its cold or warm

When she's siting in the dirt

She wears her knickers round her skirt

Blowing on an Alpine Horn.

Yodel ai ee, Yodel ai, Yodel ai ee, you little nowty bugger.

She likes to nip in't Social for some apres ski

A pint of Irish coffee or a cup of tea

With a bob hat on her head

Rayban shades to knock 'em dead

All the fellers there are on their knees. (yodel)

When its Spring she dances round the town

With flowers in her hair and her face cast down

With a pocket full of frogs

She tap dances in her clogs

And she'll give you a kiss for half a crown. (yodel)

She can ski like buggery down Parbold Hill

When the owd men see her coming it makes them ill

In her tight skiing pants

She puts them in a trance

Then she can moves in easily for the kill. (yodel)

She likes her fondue and her tartiflette

She can eat alpine dainties just like the rest

But when no-one's looking

She'll be in the backroom cooking

Black pudding, egg and bacon on a French baguette. (yodel)

She represented Wigan at the Winter Games

She skated in th'Arena with her hair in flames

With a spangly little belt

And wearing nothing else

They were inundated with insurance claims. (yodel)

So if you're stood on't slag heaps by the setting sun

And if you hear her coming then you better run

As she slaloms left and right

You won't ever win a fight

With a ski stick sticking out your bum. (yodel)

75.

China in my land. (New song)

He wears a body cam cos he's a man ready for the future,

And he knows he must retain the facts to prove he's clean.

He will be prepared for all the bruises and the sutures,

The rules are clear and the cops are mean.

Electronic dog tags, papers in his hand, number on his forehead

The electric eyes follow him wherever he has to go.

He lost some credits socialising with the wrong people

He needs to try harder its bad when credits get too low.

You have to watch what you say almost anything can be misconstrued.

If they could see what he was thinking now they'd stop him buying food.

From the rising sun Which side are you on my comrade brother,

You know if you're not with us you're against us to the very end.

We don't need cameras, cops and robots to contain you,

We do that through your friends, through your dearest friends.

Where's my iPad, where's my phone

What's my bar code for this zone

Maybe better we're not seen together

After all they're trying to control the weather.

So he lives alone in a de-organised zone somewhere in the mountains

And he lives a meagre life of fruit or roadkill in his dish

In the banquet cities they feast while the committees

Observe their eyes, they all have eyes like fish.

They took his wife and kids locked them up like pigs with no resistance.

Processed them under burning lamps.

Everywhere he looks the council spooks, vacant looks, helmeted goons in the distance.

Put them into re-education camps.

Freedom looks alive and well from distance.

Smiling faces, electronic gadgets for everyone.

As long as you follow the path of least resistance

You will hardly notice when your freedom's gone.

76.

God being Creative.

Ahv geet a lot on this week

Wi all this creatin' lark.

Neaw then, poof! Light.

Thats getten rid o yon dark.

Neaw what we goin't do wi light

Just leavin it theer's not fair.

I know! ast make up some sky

And throw in a bit o yon air.

After't th'earth ahl do moon and all't stars

I have fert do loads o them buggers.

What's that Saint Peter, do I want a brew?

Ay lad, the usual, two sugars.

Neaw for all them creatures

Ah met as well have a bit of a laugh

Throw in a few you couldn't make up

Theer a peacock, theer a giraffe!

Ahm looking forward to't Sabbath

I get a rest then for a change

Towards th'end ot week ah get maisy

I hope ah don't do nothing strange.

He were havin a pint in th'Heavens Inn

Sunday dinner and havin a rest.

Playin darts with Archangel Gabriel

This week ah've give it me best.

But ah were powfagged ah must admit

When it come to Saturday neet

Created them funny things humans

Don't worry said Gabe, it'll be reet.

77.

Crossword fatigue.

"To egg on", six across?

Five letters, I mustn't boast,

I used to be good at crosswords.

"To egg on?" I've got it, toast!

My memory is like an old computer

Slow processor and 128k

"The capitol of Kazakhstan"?

Let me think, I know!, "K"

Six letters "Made from Elderberry"

Cryptic "A bottle might please her"

"Elderberry" , something to do with wine?

Got it, must be our "Teresa"

That must be wrong I'll try another.

Two down, ends in"im"

Three letters, "A bit dopey"

Got it! Must be "Jim"

78.

Crucifix Blues.

Never felt so alone since the doggy died and the silence came

Since the news dragged me into a whirlwind of opinion and blame

Since the people became like robots and the clouds killed the sun

Since the inspiration left me like the blast of a shotgun

Blowing all the ideas into the slime on the wall

And the lost birds call in the pouring rain

Runs like black blood down a stinking drain

Never felt so blue when nothing is hurting

And the the prickly hedgerow the soft fields skirting

Points to the hill and the tree branch noose

Swaying slowly in the blackening wind

Who survives, who won, who sinned

Guilty of living in a world full of lies and clever tricks

Where the gentle go from kindness to the crucifix.

79.

"How C got over the ex"

A decided B should not be given tea.

B said to A "What have I done today?"

"You didn't follow regulation" said A with indignation.

"If you step back in line you'll get your tea on time"

"Bloody hell" said B "You can shove your bloody tea"

"Did you also withhold tea from your old boyfriend C?"

So B phoned up C and then they both agreed.

You may need your specs but B plus C divided by A equals C over X!

80.

Glad I mowed the grass and took the sun loungers in before it snowed.

Daffodils and lambs looked happy in the sun before that north wind blowed.

That little suntan upon my face looks funny now my nose is turning blue.

And the t-shirt and shorts looked better than that Parka/welly combo does on you.

I was sweating yesterday now its gloves and boots and woolly hat I fear.

A bit like Browning said; "Oh to be in England now that April's here."

81.

My son Pipkin.

My son Pipkin is so advanced

By three months old he could ballet dance.

At the Bolshoi ballet, he adorned the footlights.

I can still see his nappy sticking out of his tights.

At the age of two he had his first pint.

Went into White Lion and started a fight.

At 2 and a half he went to university.

Wrote an award winning thesis on biodiversity.

Before he could go to the toilet for a wee.

He was made director general of the BBC.

He played for Bolton Wanderers at the age of three.

Would have played for England but for his knee.

He was working for the government by the time he was four.

Chairing secret meetings behind closed doors.

I'm so proud of my son Pipkin, what a wonderful little lad.

Hope he don't turn out to be a lying bastard like his dad.

82.

The Fay.

I met a fay thing in the lane last night

No wings, a tiny lady glowing bright.

She did not speak but talked to me,

With soundless content of her eyes.

So very old, she was so young,

Attended by a flock of fireflies.

Brittle mind words to my soul,

As far-off thunder groaned its roll.

She floated feared into the ground,

Cast silver spell dew all around,

And then I knew that lucky me,

To be the only one to see,

What others scorn and misperceive,

I met upon that springtime eve.

83.

A cloud of whizzing midges

Spin within a sphere of light.

Murmurations of starlings

3D calculus the night.

The buzzard floats an ellipse

Surveys circles without blinking.

I struggle with my Maths

They just do it without thinking.

84.

Car parked under Anglezarke - new song. (don't listen if you are already down!)

He smoked the painted sunset through a little cigar.

Threw the last remains through the window of his car.

Parked up under Anglezarke with his soul on fire.

Watched the twinkling road lights come on over Lancashire.

He could see the distant sea swallow up the sun.

Tasted the kick of the little cigar and lit another one.

Three litre Diamond White crumpled into a roll.

Nine, ninety nine vodka took the burden off his soul.

Darkness was descending, inside and outside the car.

It had become never ending, how had things come so far.

Biro and sheet of A4 on the passenger seat.

Empty bottle and crumpled cans dancing round his feet.

Dear Comrade, Where were you when I needed you most.

Seems like all my hopes and dreams have misted into a ghost.

That was all that was written, well what made any sense.

Nothing left of value, nothing of innocence.

Black lorries thundered along the distant M61.

Blazing and blaring the world of uncaring, he missed every single one.

85.

A Keaw Yed in Paris.

Pies are nowt special in Paris.

Un th'architecture's a bit dreary.

Apart from that copy o't Blackpool tower,

I were a bit disappointed and weary.

I couldn't find a pint of Holts bitter,

And mi french were inadequate for't locals.

So I geet up on stage wi a pint of wine,

An give 'em a touch of mi vocals.

I did th'owd favourite Wild Rover,

At th'end that were met with just silence.

Cheeky french buggers I thowt,

If I'd stayed theer there met have been violence.

So I wandered deawn Champs Elysees,

On mi own, wi mi pint, by the Seine.

Un a thowt I met as well be in Howfen,

Th'only difference here, its warmer, this rain.

86.

The poor tortured souls, so noble in death.

Saint Catherine on a wheel they took her last breath.

Saint Eulalia rolled down a hill,

In a barrel of knives her poor body to kill.

Saint Sebastian shot full of arrows, beaten with clubs,

Washed their hands in bloody washtubs.

Saint Lucy the proud men took out her eyes,

But eyeless they did not realise,

As she looked round the room,

In that place of her doom,

She was embarrassed to see such of man.

Submitted to bear what others will do,

A humble acceptance of what others will do.

What human excess becomes so monumental,

Whose greatest pleasure is hurting the gentle.

That is the pain that made her sightless eyes cry.

Such a thing, such a thought, just before you die.

87.

These beans are well past their sell-by date, don't worry they'll be fine.

They don't go off when they're in a tin. But it says 1989!

That is not a problem, just warm them up.You'll never tell.

There's some soup here from the seventies! Well just warm that up as well.

These sell by dates are a conspiracy by a government rotten to the core.

They want you to throw everything away.Then go out and buy some more.

Speaking of rotten to the core, what's that weird thing in the fridge.

Looks like it is something that just fell off as bridge.

Don't be so soft it will be good. I'll cook it for our tea.

Well good luck with that, looks like beans and soup for me.

There's a tin at the back all gone green, looks like its covered in satin.

And wait a minute, look at that, the sell by date's in Latin!

Maybe we can let that one go but do not touch the rest.

Sometimes food needs times to settle to bring out all its best.

There's some Christmas pickles in a jar stuck together all gone blue.

Oh they are fine they, made them like that in 1962.

I ordered a skip, emptied the cupboards I'm not eating all this shite!

But I kept back a few tins for valuation, Sotheby's coming round tonight.

88.

Don't mention that! Don't go there.

There are some subjects now we just can't debate.

Please understand just by bringing it up.

You may be guilty of causing hate.

No, I don't want any trouble, I have no axes to grind,

Just thought talking is good, we could clear the air.

You need educating, things have changed.

We'll give you instructions but don't you dare.

So I went to the party, stood there with a drink.

Chattering and chinking, I stood in the gloom.

Bloody hell! Is this Chester zoo?

Never seen so many elephants in one room.

89.

"In these times of compassion, where conformity's in fashion"

Let's all conform, it's the right thing to do.

It's easy and everyone's doing it now.

Surely you don't want the others to hate you.

Just do as your told and don't start a row.

Follow the new rules, they are easy to find.

Just turn on the telly and not just the news.

The new way of living/obeying is obvious,

Do not detract and get in your queues.

Follow the masses, the numbers know best.

You don't want to seem like a belligerent old fool.

Listen to the leaders, the experts, the media,

Don't think for yourself that is so, so old school.

Follow the powers, they know where to go.

They'll tell you everything you need to know.

90.

A weasel is living in the bonfire.

Leaps and runs and stops,

Hardly possible to follow her speed.

On back legs then squeaks,

And slips into her lair.

Turns with one eye wary till I go.

Little wild beast I love your vicious beauty.

I must dissect the jungle bit by bit,

Ensuring she has gone before it burns.

She squeaks again and turns,

And disappears into her labyrinth.

(Not my photo as it is too quick for me to catch!)

91.

Let's make a fire and sit by it,

Under the soundless sky.

Sparks will float to join the stars,

As the western daylight dies.

We could be wedged in the city,

With taxis and neon lights.

Clubs and pubs and bouncing noise,

In the man made paradise.

But here we are sat by strawberry embers,

Under grey, black crumbling wood.

Singular silence, barn owl patrols,

The field's edge and all is good.

92.

I've got a talking horse - New song.

Losing your love is like losing the end of the sellotape.

You can't feel it on the roll, you can't see it on the roll,

No matter how you scrape.

I got a talking horse, she tells me the truth.

Plus she can see for miles, when she's standing on the roof.

How does she get up there, she's been on a course.

She's an SAS private eye, I've got a talking horse.

The milk man came today and you asked him inside.

Why do you have to deny, what have you got to hide.

I know you like to mix and love social intercourse.

I may be out at work, but I got a talking horse.

We had the builders in, they got a lot to do.

But they always down their tools when you make them a brew.

Why do you have to dress that way for the labour force.

How do I know all this, I got a talking horse.

You went to the bedroom you said to rest your head.

But I heard a different story, the horse was under the bed.

If she can't always be watching you twenty four.

She sub-contracts her duties to that tom cat from next door.

You think that you are it, some hot bitch of society.

But I got me a snitch of the equine variety.

You say you're true to me and you don't want the divorce.

I don't need a private eye, I've got a talking horse.

93.

THE FIRST TIME.

The first time must be perfect for a couple new like us.

No fumbling around in cheap hotels or the back seat of a bus.

With mutual respect and love, lust can be kept at bay.

We can plan it, make it perfect, for us our special day.

We're not like the others who can't wait to jump in bed.

False promises and compliments just to get misled.

It's not just sex, it's making love with the one love of all time.

A perfect union, innocent, spotless and sublime.

The first time must be perfect, then fate played its cruel tricks.

We did it in a lay-by on the A66.

94.

I am man and moped.

I am going for some milk.

I will never change.

Nor will others of my ilk.

49cc between my legs.

Two pedals for my feet.

Dressed in TT leathers.

I'm a hunky piece of meat.

My face is red from windburn.

Not embarrassment.

With my helmet and my goggles.

I'm a groovy kind of gent.

Girls may look and giggle.

As I putter putter by.

But they secretly desire me.

And don't even realise.

I love my little Honda.

I keep it by the bed.

Man and machine together.

Both thoroughbred.

I am man and moped.

I spend my nights alone.

My body is a temple.

Six foot three of skin and bone.

95.

All the great men - New Microsong.

All the great men have all gone.

Stalin, Hitler every one.

Idi Amin, Chairman Mao,

Whatever shall we all do now.

Enver Pasha, Ghengis Khan,

Leopold the Belgian man.

Vlad the Impaler, Cromwell's reign,

Torquemada, Tamerlane.

Attilla the Hun, Caligula,

Javed Iqbal, Yang Xinai,

Franco, Shipman, Chikatillo,

Did Lenin sleep well on the pillow.

Ivan the Terrible did a lot,

Mussolini and Pol Pot.

John Wayne Gacy, Jeffrey Dahmer,

Jack the Ripper, such a charmer,

Pedro Lopez, Ted Bundy too,

Sorry if I missed a few.

They led the world a merry dance.

Maybe time to give the girls a chance.

96.

She lived upon a rock, wester than the west.

Surrounded by the blast of the Atlantic.

Old slate crumbling croft, perched upon the cliff,

No telly, but her garden views fantastic.

She is older than she was and younger than that too

Sea shine bleached her hair and creased her skin.

She never used her mirror, nothing to see there.

Her beauty once on show and now within.

They dragged her kicking from her little world,

Health and safety, council knocked it down.

The best thing for her, poor crazy thing,

A sheltered home in the comfort of a town.

Now she sits in silence in her room.

They make sure she has everything she needs.

While the white tipped waves blow hard across her cliff,

And the sad faced moon looks down upon the weeds.

97.

Damn that cold east wind

It blew my house to pieces.

The chimney pot, the satellite dish,

Gas meter box blown in the ditch.

The gutter end, the broken tiles,

Recycling contents lost for miles.

I went out dressed in hat and fleeces.

Now all is well and all is fixed.

While sunset plays its peaceful tricks.

98.

Average guitar player.

I wish I could play guitar like Segovia,

Sarge Frampton or Pete Townsend.

I started off with G and soon figured out D

But I've been in A minor wilderness since then.

A barred high E Minor really makes my fingers sore

But after all what are capos for!

I'm an average guitar player, there are millions just like me.

We start learning quick, then we hit the brick wall of ability.

We're in a rush to get out there to show what we can do.

Then the laziness just sets in and we go and make a brew.

I cover up my inadequacies by hitting the bugger loud.

I'm an average guitar player thank god that's still allowed.

That Tommy Emmanuel from Australia he really gets on my wick.

Whizzing up and down with a smile on his face, how can anyone play so quick!

Jimi Hendrix, Brian May, Eric Clapton, Stevie Ray

Mato Sica, Jimmy Page, heroes of the guitar age.

Taking fretboards to the brink while I still do my plinkety plink.

I'm an average guitar player but I've been working in lockdown.

Writing like a nutter with art from the gutter and I'm coming to your town!

99.

He loved it, that Martin guitar,

He went to London to buy it.

He could play like a whizz anyway,

But they let him sit and try it.

He brought it home on the train,

To play for his beloved to hear.

But she didn't care, she was having an affair,

And a move up in career.

When he found out he picked her up

By the neck and smashed out her life.

Splinters and strings and unplayed things,

The guitar, not his wife.

100.

The Japanese troops would be hiding in the cushions,

Their cannon stuck on th'hoover with a wire.

Viking and Apaches had joined up for this battle.

The British army camped out near the fire.

I could use the dog and cat as lookouts.

If only they would do as they were told.

Then move my soldiers up to th'arm of the chair,

And then the glorious battle would enfold.

I was pretending to listen to the history,

The priest was droning reading from his book.

I was gazing at the sky tears on the window,

When he gave me that scary cold eyed look.

The clock was ticking minutes just like hours.

I carved my name with biro on't desk lid.

Not be long n I'll be back home with me soldiers.

We'll find where them pesky Japanese have hid.

101.

Time ticking, another day lost

For the young ones.

Days that can't come back again.

Their days worth a hundred of mine.

No friends around, no playing.

I understand the loss and the crying.

I understand the caring and the giving.

The government can't stop people dying.

But they can certainly stop young people living.

102.

Who will cry for Angela tonight.

Beaten and tortured to death.

The last of her daily 9 litres strong cider,

Still stinking on her last breath.

Or cry for the girls 13 and 14.

She welcomed into her home.

Already addicted like her to the booze.

Even so young the syndrome,

And spiral addiction reality blurring

They smashed her and stamped her to hell.

What a life, what a poor life, ending like that,

After 39 years who can tell.

What hopeless existence drove her to this.

Call the murderers just heartless scum.

But maybe through mist of being constantly pissed.

They murdered what they would become.

103.

The first upward curve on the graph of love,

Everything is going in the right direction.

The signs, the waves that make you think.

The product will be love perfection.

Then the sex and why? co-ordinates,

Result in a disastrous peak

After that its all down hill,

And you'll be off at a tangent next week.

104.

Little Star - New Song.

Shine bright little star, share your light with me.

You are insignificant in the wondrous galaxy.

But you will still be burning when I have lost the fight.

So Shine bright little star, shine on me tonight.

Don't want to be part of any totalitarianism.

And if I was religious I'd probably start a schism.

So it looks like it is just you and me tonight under the blue.

10 million light years away and a sense of humour too.

You know if all the humans disappeared in the middle of the night.

Old planet earth would just carry on, everything would be alright.

We are only important in terms of our own human interaction.

Thinking we were special in some way maybe an overreaction.

I know there's a lot of good people in the world tonight.

People who care and spend their lives trying to make things right.

So God bless everyone and don't live too dangerously.

Share your light, no matter how bright, don't take yourself too seriously.

105.

Monday morning poem reflecting on misguided body enhancements.

I wish I had never had Kylie Minogue's face

Tattooed on my left buttock in Bahrain.

Now the ravages of time, ink fading, wrinkles have combined.

It looks more like Rod Stewart on cocaine.

There is nothing wrong with Rod, to some he's still a god.

But there are fans who act like psychopaths.

And I must avoid the stares of homophobic bears.

When taking off my trunks in Atherton Baths.

Regret is not a word I use a lot these days.

But those lip implants I thought would bring me luck.

Have retained their superfluity while my face an incongruity

Left me resembling a Hammer Horror Donald Duck.

The word Ludo is tattooed on my private part.

Whyever I had it done I'll never know.

But on holiday you just don't think and then things begin to shrink.

I could have sworn it used to say LLandudno.

106.

I feel sorry for birds sat on't roof wi nowt to do.

I saw one yesterday on't wet ridge tile reet fed up.

Ahve often thowt about being a bird and being free

But when I seed yon mon he looked no freer than me.

I wonder what goes through their little yeds.

Having wings an aw that business wi their eggs.

They must look at me like a great big lump of meat.

Stumbling abeawt on me slow long spindly legs.

You have the power of flight! God give it ya!

Have a jet areawnd instead o feelin sorry for thisel.

He just looked at me and me at him.

Then both went back to our own private hell.

107.

Revelation on a toilet door. New song.

I found out about the facts of life from the back of toilet doors.

Killing time in Bolton where the women are all whores.

At least that's what one door poet said pouring out his life.

I wondered if he ever could forgive his cousin and his wife.

The art was basic, graphic drawn with knife or ball point pen.

No Relationships/Sex education in my school back then.

So I had to read the information and work out in my head.

Whether Mavis from Astley Bridge truly did the things they said.

But the bulk of their shared wisdom really opened my eyes full wide.

What some men did to other men I had never realised.

The first time that I read it, it scrambled up my brain.

So later I had to go back in and read it all again.

Having led a sheltered childhood I was shaken to the core.

My pure love affair with Mary Poppins was shattered on that door.

I walked off Moor Lane station round the streets and in the rain.

I would never look at men and women quite the same again.

I had a Tanner and a ha'penny got some Kayli and a Spanish.

Sat on a bench and wondered when that sordid world would vanish.

The sun burst through the rain with the puzzled clouds departing.

It was 1964 and the whole world was just starting.

108.

Ghost Bride.

I spied a wench the other night in the desolate countryside.

A walking down a darkling road in the trappings of a bride.

White veil, white dress and dainty shoes besmirched with splats of mud.

And on her hand a wedding ring all covered up with blood.

Kind sir, she said, can you aid me, her face a snowy sheet,

But oh her eyes, her lifeless eyes, black and wet as peat.

She sat beside me on the journey silent, cold and still.

Where must you go fair maiden for I wish you no ill.

Her spindly finger pointed thus to the empty road ahead.

And we drove in vacuous silence and a sense of growing dread.

Then there it was the mansion dark with windows glowing red.

And all about the garden walked the figures of the dead.

I looked across to let her out and a terror gripped my throat.

Forsooth the seat was empty save for a ten pound note.

I spun around and drove like hell to leave the fiendish scene.

Last time I do a taxi job on bloody halloween.

109.

I got off the jumbo at Murtala Muhammed hotter than a Bedouin's jockstrap.

I easily walked to the front of the queue while the others were taking a nap.

A little soldier with a hundred medals pointed at me with his cane.

"Get to the back of the queue" he said, I thought I was going insane.

He tapped my chest with his brass ferrule and repeated his command.

"Why" I said as another soldier said "You need to move, you understand?"

So I walked a bit back and they turned their attention to other important things.

I was the only white face in the long black line, I kept looking at his fists full of rings.

When they let me through I had a taxi waiting to drive through Lagos at night.

My poor driver stopped at illegal road blocks by Nigerian soldiers high as kites.

They asked me what do I bring for them from England and Her Majesty.

I said "Greetings and good luck!" was I living in a fantasy!

One pushed a machine gun through the window bad whisky on his breath.

He said "You do not want to die tonight my friend" in a taxi, here? my death!

They took me to the compound at Awolowa road let me go like a wild baboon.

And I slept in safety in a cooled bed under the grinning African moon.

110.

There was a house on the road

A pond across from it.

White line painted curve.

That is where he died.

On a motorbike.

That slid in the side

Of the brick

From a slick

Makes you sick

Now his skeleton dances

On the steam of the pond

When a restless crow shivers

And the evening is wrong.

111.

Hey You Ferret Face!

Hey You! Ferret face, yeah you, I'm talkin to you.

Have you been causing trouble again.

Cos you've bugger all else to do.

Stop in and play with your rattle.

Look at yourself in a concave lens.

Yeah you, ferret face, no wonder you have no friends.

Hey thee, snot rag, yeah thee, I'm talking to thee.

Are you still sellin' poison to t'kids,

After you start 'em off on't free.

Go't church and pray to thi maker

Cos if I see thee sellin reawnd here.

Ahl bury thee under't midden, no-one'll miss thee, no fear.

Hey you Mrs Gobshite, yeah you I'm talking to you.

Driving too fast when there's kids in't road.

Like a fly with an arse of blue.

Slow down, you're not in a hurry

I've seen you move when you get out o't car

Drive at the same speed you slobber abeawt, you're not a bloody film star.

Hey you, nice considerate person, yeah you I'm talkin to you.

Nobody takes the time to say thanks.

When you help those worse off than you.

They give MBE's and OBE's and knighthoods to some right plonkers

When you put others before yourself some might think you'r bonkers.

I know you're not, I know you're not.

Most people are good and caring and some are little snots.

Here's to the ones who take the time

To help others less lucky than them.

And when these bad times are all over we'll all be better friends.

112.

Black Snow.

The snow turned black

As it blew in sheets through the sooty burning land.

Falling feathery ebony flakes,

From the frozen maker's hand.

The deep black snow banks held my dreams

From the cauldrons of banality.

I looked outside when I awoke

To the grey slush of reality.

113.

Be careful when you're changing things.

Not every thing needs changing.

Make sure good heart does not get lost,

With your political re-arranging.

The hippest wines consumed by minds,

In Knightsbridge or Greenwich village.

May not travel well to poorer towns

And watch out for the spillage.

114.

No don't do it like that, do it like me.

It's not enough to care and love you see.

If you don't do it just like me.

You are not of the fraternity.

Can't you see what we say is true?

Then not to walk in our same shoe!

Not to do the things just like we do.

That may end up dangerous for you.

Its so annoying when you don't comply.

Your loss of freedom - oh my.

Birds are free under the sky.

What are you trying to do - die?

115.

Funfair (new song - X rated)

I'll take you to the peak of the Big Dipper.

I'll shoot your target down with my air gun.

I'd better not mention the tunnel of love.

To be fair we never had so much fun.

Can I put my penny in your game slot.

I'm hoping for two cherries and a bar.

Don't be shy my coconuts need knocking off.

Bang me with your dirty dodgem car.

Can I have a mouthfull of your candy floss.

For your double top I'll give the darts a throw.

Let's go up and down on the Speedway.

The louder you scream the faster we will go.

Let's have a bumpy ride on the Ghost train.

I'll raise your spirits just you wait and see.

I'll race you to the end of the Big One.

First prize if you get there before me.

Wrap your legs around me on the Log Flume.

If you get wet then blame it all on me.

What a night we're having on the funfair.

Worth the admission I hope that you agree.

116.

Bobby - new song about an old bloke with his dog on the streets.

The pavement was hard but the coffee was gold

A jet left its sign in the sky pushing west.

The layers of coats couldn't keep out the cold.

But the steam from the cup! and the smile did the rest.

Venus still twinkling as the morning star rose,

On Bobby and me my little four legged satnav.

You sleep in my jacket, you eat from my hands.

Don't die tonight Bobby you're all that I have.

Each town has the concrete, each town has the rain.

The doorways are few and their all taken up.

But Bobby and me we'll find solace tonight.

A bottle for me biscuits in his paper cup.

We're in today Bobby she just gave me a note.

Special biscuits for you and the usual for me.

It'll be different tomorrow, we'll start something new.

Come on Bobby just you wait and see.

117.

You are just an insignificant speck in the time and mass of the cosmos

Yet you invented beans on toast and timeshares in Torremolinos.

Your little life is close to nowt next to the lifespan of the comets.

But you still watch Tipping Point in your onesy eating cheesy Wotsits.

The nuclear sun sees your life as nothing but an annoying little zit

Vera's been asking you to marry her for 14 years and still you can't commit.

It takes ninety three billion light years to cross the Galaxies.

Yet you wasted three quarters of an hour discussing offside technicalities.

But when you mended that old blokes car and didn't ask for any pay.

And smiled at someone for a second, that really made their day.

Trapped in time and trapped in a life where things pass by so quickly.

There's nothing wrong with shaving your legs if you think they're getting prickly.

118.

2021 resolutions.

We're not talking to that Mrs Turner, not my friend anymore.

When we were all out clapping on a Thursday night

She was hiding behind't front door.

And that mate of yours who voted Brexit, He can do one for me.

When we're having paella and chips he won't be coming round for tea.

All your left wing Labour loony pals with pink bracelets on their wrists,

Think they're all goody goodies, bloody Communists!

That Tory voting extreme right winger Tom can kiss my bum.

And that goes for all the white supremacists all over Atherton.

That swine in Tesco with no mask on, he killed my uncle Bill.

And I wont be leaving bloody NHS any money in my will.

I think your son's in Antifa I've seen the way he skulks about.

And that Mrs Brown's a Nazi, she never puts recycling out.

My wife's a non-transgender woman but I haven't told her yet.

She will accept it gracefully, she will! You wanna bet.

Leave windows open to kill the virus said that nutter Janet.

Leave windows open wit th'heating on that won't save the bloody planet.

Aye and leave poor Lewis Hamilton alone, he's had a difficult past,

Chased by all them racists, no wonder he drives so fast.

We're supposed to be in tier 4, your sister's been out twice.

She's a homicidal maniac and I thought that she were nice.

I've had to turn the telly off, not sure which news to watch.

That bloody woman's out again! I've started my stopwatch.

119.

Your loneliness is yours alone

A bleak no other comprehends

Sitting at a table with an empty cup of coffee

In the middle of a myriad of friends

Your footsteps walk the unique path

Though millions have passed this way before

Your feelings as you put that little key

In the silence behind your own front door.

120.

Everyone's a singer now

All the world's a stage

Famous for fifteen minutes

Escaping from the cage

The cage of watching others

Be the one they want to see

Screaming at the stars

In a way of feeling free

Everyone's a soap star

Their episode of fame

Emotionally describing

Their role in the game

The game of life can be hard

Shouldn't be but it is

Escape from it with booze and drugs

Or starring in showbiz.

121.

Pass me the shotgun Ellie-May

The Government boys are here

Taking away our freedoms

For the greater good so I hear

They use fear to intimidate you

Then they make you step in line

And they say its your moral duty

And it works nearly every time

You can't own any property

The elite need to dip their beaks

Put you in a camp, inject your arm

Loopy juice every thirteen weeks

The World Economic Forum

Hold the keys to the globalist dream

Your freedom's a minor encumbrance

You need to be part of the team

You and I are not clever enough

Davos suits will take care of the queries

Get in line for the good of all

Stop thinking conspiracy theories

122.

New song "Days of torrents"

Well I'm sitting in my kitchen and the sun is going to bed

leaving streaks of light across the sky, horizon clothed in red

And there's wars and hurt and arguments

Bad feelings and worries galore

But I can't hold onto that no more.

I joined this river when it was young and fast

As it slowed and grew so did I

Now the days of torrents and turbulence

Are long gone by.

I have sunk back into the shadows where the cold invisible rain

Cools my racing senses and makes me calm again

And watching the last rays of the sun from the darkness of my door

Give thanks to God for a lovely day and I'm wishing there'll be more.

Now I cannot fight in other fights and I cannot right the wrongs

Neither tossing and turning in my bed or raging in my songs

So here I sit in the cold evening arrows rusting in the quiver

And I'm glad to be alive just now near the sea on my life's river.

When I was young like that sparking stream I scraped the rocks and stone

Fighting and laughing, hating and loving, and now I'm all alone

I've gone slow and I'm near the sea, river's curling its last bend

And its calmer now and its beautiful, thank God from start to end.

123.

Frond on Pond.

With your mercury depths and the darkness and the mud

To your bright crystal water where the pond skaters scud

And your lily pads and your flowers in bud

No cathedral has more silent thunder

With your weeds and reeds where the sunlight dims

Into your expanse where the fishes swim

And your dragonfly hovers with his perfect wings

So few gaze upon your wonder

Little pond in blessed magic

Peaceful place away from tragedy

My warehouse eyes my Arabian drums

Should I leave them by your shores

As we wait by Summer's doors.

124.

If your teeth were made of diamonds, your back was made of steel

Your shelf life would be longer but could you really feel

The wonderment of being alive for just today

Our transient existence in an ageing precious way.

If you had so much money that you needed fifty banks

And security was provided by armoured cars and tanks

If ladies swooned, men got jealous every time that you were seen

And your face adorned the cover of the coolest magazine

If you were so important with your fortune and your fame

In the bathroom and the toilet would all that be the same?

If they replaced all your vital bits ten times to keep you going

And they kept you in a sterile room with pure air conditioned blowing

And every germ and disease was on the outside of your door

Would anybody really care when you were finally no more.

125.

Moaning wind you fill me with insouciance

Moaning wind your becoming a bloody nuisance

The beast from the east, you've been groaning three days flat

Even flatulence from curry doesn't last as long as that

May the isobars start twisting, may the low pressure shift

A bit of calm and sunshine would make my spirits lift

Bugger off to Sweden if you get my bloody drift - moaning wind.

 Moaning wind you come from the land of grizzly bears

 Moaning wind its pretty up in Scotland please go there

 Talk about repetitive, give it a bloody rest

 You just blew a busy robin off its little nest

 Wherever you are going please get their a bit quicker

 Your making me palpitate and I've got a dodgy ticker

 I'm thinking of anaesthetising myself with hard liquor - moaning wind

Moaning wind, you're the opposite of a sedative

Moaning wind, your melody is extremely repetitive

If I could put you in a rocket I would blast you off to mars

I've met more interesting subjects unconscious in bars

You're meteorologically insignificant you're a three on the Beaufort scale

Any self respecting weatherman wouldn't refer to you as a gale

If they were selling winds you'd be half price in a sale - moaning wind.

Moaning wind, your giving me incontinence

Moaning wind, please visit some other continents

On a scale of one to fifty you're a minus fifty three

I'd give you a piece of my mind but I'm going to make my tea

You Moaning Wind!

126.

When I first started drinkin a pint were one and ten

Bar was made of brass and oak and glass, but that were then

Milly thin owd waitress could move at speed o light

Tray full o drinks and crisps and a needle with a big eye

Thowd men outside on't thaunches flat caps and smoking

Coal eyeliner not washed out chunnerin and jokin

Pubs were magic palaces honky tonk piano playin

Landlord smart wi't white ironed shirt collar stiff and frayin

Darts were heavy fat brass bombs squeezed into't treble twenty

Racing pages covered in scribble by't local cognoscenti

Victorian toilets white and gold, urinals target bee

Cig end floating into't grid wi't disinfectant pee

Heroes proppin't bar up wi hands like gauntlet leather

Spiv man in his three piece suit trilby wi a feather

Not a telly, not a juke box, not a one armed bandit

I could go out suppin neaw in't pub, but I don't think I could stand it.

127.

Ah to be in England now that Spring is here.

Equality and sharing wealth, these values we hold dear.

In Kensington and Chelsea you can live till 95.

In Blackpool if you're 68 you're lucky to be alive.

128.

If there was a war would you want your son to fight.

Or your husband or your brother even if the cause seemed right.

If there was a war would you want your son to go

Offer up his life in foreign lands for people you don't know.

If the war was very far away and the blame remained unclear,

When political media says we must, would you want to keep him near.

Or if the fight was close to home in Italy or France,

Would you dress him in his uniform to join the bloody dance.

Oh in those shuttered rooms in the corridors of power

You will never know what has been said, would you give your son's last hour.

If there was a war with propaganda raging round

Calls of white feather cowardice would you join the battle sounds

Would you kiss him on the cheek, farewell party, drinks in hand

We must do what we must do we must try to understand.

If there was a war could you find a hiding place

Far away from all the killing, all the hurt and the disgrace.

129.

Three storms on't trot!

Upsetting me psyche.

Rattlin' all't slates

Me no likey.

Drips reawnd't winders

Grids blocked wi mud.

Ditch all oer't road.

Not bloody good.

First it were Dudley

Then bloody Eunice

Sky all same't colour

Not bloody blueness.

Neaw wiv geet Franklin

Fresh eawt ot th'Atlantic.

Thanks a lot pal.

Dogs gooin frantic.

Three storms on't trot.

Flyin oer't border.

Global warming?

Eawt of order!

130.

Fading, peeling virus warnings on the station platform floor.

Wind blows through the tunnels and another bit disappears.

Time moves on, people move on, nature doesn't care.

Old posters blistered in the sun, long dead stars faces.

Abandoned buildings crumbling, antique irrelevant graffiti

Time moves on, people move on, nature doesn't care.

WW2 fire signs painted on the old brick gables almost invisible

Overgrown graves of heroes, names nobody remembers

Closed pits, winding gear silhouette, shakes at sunset

Factories, mills where people worked for pennies

Redundant soldiers sleeping rough in the park

High society party dripping gold and giggling in Knightsbridge

Time moves on, people move on, nature doesn't care.

131.

I saw life through a cowboy's eyes.

Riding down into a dusty red canyon sunset.

Planning revenge on that owder lad at school.

Hot lead from from my Colt between his eyes.

Slap my leg and gallop up Church street.

One day I may really have a horse.

Raise my stetson school cap "G'mornin maam"

Drink some gritty water from my canteen.

It doesn't rain so much in cowboy films.

Make a lasso from my mother's washing line.

Maybe rope some wanderin steer before sundown.

Fix a twig fire down in the dry gulch near't bonk.

Cook some beans and coffee, steak on a stick.

One day they'll maybe let me into a saloon

Drink some whisky, pow wow with an Indian on the way home.

132.

What is misinformation Dad?

There are just two sorts my dear.

First there's the stuff that is just not true,

Then there's truth they don't want you to hear.

So some lies are truth are they Dad,

According to the powers that be.

Yes my love in the good old days

We'd look for truth from the BBC.

Now it has become more elusive,

It still exists but it's omitted and rare.

There's truth that gets shown to them, me and you,

Then the truth hard to find, but it's there.

133.

Today turned into drizzle soup

Flattening morning optimism

Rooks squabbling in the ivied oak

Seen through zinc sky raindrop prism

S.A.D the disease of February

Thinking Winter can ne'er be beat

Then there beneath the thorn hedgerow

A thousand snowdrops at my feet

134.

Don't worry, you're just one of the little people.

Don't think too much, you'll just get confused.

Please follow the official lines that you are given.

Even if sometimes you think you're being abused.

It's not advisable to use your God given brain.

That's all being done for you by the powers above.

Remember they are doing it for the greater good.

Don't trouble your little mind about it love.

If you know sometimes you think this doesn't make sense,

You've just been misinformed by conspiracy theories.

The truth is easier from the Government and the media.

Use the fact checkers, they will resolve all of your queries.

135.

Painted Princess of Shiffnall Street. (new song)

It's not that long ago when you could be seen

Playing hopscotch in the cobbled back streets

Dirty hair, threadbare clothes so thin

You couldn't keep out the cold with no socks on your feet.

Now painted princess of Shiffnall street

How did it come to this

Selling your love for the filthy drug

To the gruesome man who stinks of booze and piss

I wish I could give you just a hug.

Your eyes look forty and your seventeen

Sitting on a crash barrier, putting on lipstick

A futureless day, street light come on

Here's a tenner from a man who makes you sick.

Some diamond white and a laugh with the girls

Turn off reality for a while

Then out in the drizzle and leaning in cars

Through broken teeth you put on that smile.

Your life is over and it hasn't begun

Make-up running in the pouring rain

I wish you were that little girl you were

So you could maybe start all over again.

136.

Follow the science! That is what they all say.
One of the popular phrases in use today.
Splitting the atom, what a marvellous find.
But politicians had something else on their mind.
Hitler, he used the best scientists available.
Mao Zedong employed only the capable.
When the surgeons were dissecting bits off poor jews.
Following the science was the Nazi front news.
You may be able to extrapolate negative zero
But a Masters in Maths doesn't make you a hero.
Now of course I'm not saying all scientists are bad.
The majority amazingly good I might add.
But "follow the science" phrase gets me annoyed
It depends by whom scientists are employed
Their pure work results in advance and invention
But just think about the political intention.

137.

There's uncounted unique images
There's a billion unwritten songs
They are flying in imagination sky
But they don't exist for long
It is up to you to catch them
But only when they pass your way
You can't force them or invent them
You can't make them come and play
So be patient and be ready
To receive them from the blue
That perfect song, that image
One moment comes to you
Then you write it and you play it
And then you must let it go
Cos it was never yours you know
You just received it, let it go.

138.

Beer cans in the bluebells
Pizza boxes down the lane
Looks like we've been honoured
By roving visitors again.
Here in the fragrant morning

Under the warming blue
At one with the trees and flowers
I never think of sniffing glue.
Here in the brittle morning
A perfect robin bravely sits
While they lie snoring in their stench
The boring little gits.

139.

She heard the Oscar winner's lament,
And she knew just what it meant:
Put on your coat, turn off your central heating.
She sat shivering in the dark
Thinking of his words so stark.
How kind of him to share his time so fleeting.
He walked down off the stage,
He was really all the rage,
Back slaps and champagne flutes, a crazy scene.
In his four thousand dollar suit,
He threw his Oscar in the boot,
Then rode home in his five litre limousine.

A Christmas tale of Harrock Hill.

Part one.

Countless tons of water in the sky floating above Lancashire. Dripping, pouring, leaking and sheeting across the field. Gutters overflowing and the ditches gurgling and flushing with water the colour of milky tea. In the stable to get some firewood for the evening. I moved some larger logs and saw something shining protruding from the bark of one old oak log.

I took an axe and split the log several times until it revealed a metal disc embedded in the fibres of the wood. With a knife I retrieved the disc. It appeared to be a gold coin with a strange inscription. I turned it over in my hand. "Recant!" boomed a disembodied voice that shook the very fabric of the building. I dropped the coin in shock and silence came in an instant within leaving only the sound of blowing rain across the stable door blown shut behind me. I gathered up some firewood and trudged back to the house collar up against the elements.

Awake at two in the morning I could not stop the memories of the gold disc and the awful booming voice. I lay on my back in silence until I could bear it no more. I looked through the windows across the field with lakes of mist hanging inches from the ground. Across the field in the distance the oak trees stood stark, their black branches and twigs pointing to a barren moon.

Slipping open the catch on the stable door I entered and saw the floor illuminated by the moon. There on the concrete floor amid the twigs and sawdust the gold coin lay bathed in white light.........

A Christmas tale. part 2.

Not wanting to touch the coin again I covered it with a rag and brought it into the house and placed it by the fire on a ledge built into the old hearth. I unfolded the rag and could make out some letters eroded by time and fingertips. "Eliz" and "Regin" were visible. I left it there untouched until morning.

Only a few days from Christmas we had been to do our shopping to prepare. Memories of the unsettling events buried under a blanket represented by traffic, crowds and noise.Yesterday's rain had turned to sleet and a bitter wind whistled round the corner of the house. As we let ourselves in a yellow glow was shining under the kitchen door.

There on the long oak table were set two brass candelabra with a dozen burning candles in each. In that soft light were displayed all the festive foods and jolly decorations. A huge roasted turkey and all the trimmings to go with it sat on glistening brass platters. Holly and ivy and red berries set off the scene. Then I noticed on the perimeter of the main plate read the words. "Take this token that I freely forgive thee and others that have been accessory to my death". Who could have done this in our house when we were out?

On the ledge near the now dead fire the gold coin glowed. I picked it up and a gentle voice whispered "No, my lord". The crack and whoosh of a slamming door sucking the air out of the room into a silent vacuum introduced a face at the window. The lights went out.

I went to fiddle with the consumer unit hoping it wasn't a power cut when the lights came back on. The table was bare and the room was very cold....The face at the window was gone.

A Christmas tale. Part 3.

On an evening walk with the dogs, just as the sun began to sink behind Harrock hill, the snow began to drift down from the sky like sugar stealers. Up higher the snow was sticking and the moon rose over Winter Hill in the distance. The seven orange lights on the 1000 foot mast shimmering. Although Harrock hill is only 515ft. tall it is the last high ground before the Lancashire plain that stretches to the Irish sea. So from this vantage point you can see all the way to the Lake District and Snowdonia and the Peak District. Nice to see smoke curling from slumbering cottage chimneys and marker lights of a distant A road.

As the lane became steeper the trees thickened to our right. That is when I saw him. A hunched figure moving from tree to tree in the gloom. Lottie, my dog, began to bark and slipped her collar and ran like the wind into the dark woods. I ran after her following her footprints in the snow.

Under the fir trees the snow could not fall and her prints disappeared. I saw the hunched figure ahead. "Have you seen my dog, please!", No reply and he moved away. I put my hand on his shoulder "My dog?". He turned to face me and I saw him up close. he looked ancient: sunken blue eyes, a toothless mouth but the most striking thing was a faded blue tattoo across his cheeks and nose spelling the word "PAENITEBIT". His strength was astonishing! With one hand he pushed me onto the ground.

Looking down at me he bent over, slaver slithering from his maw, and said "You have found it". He shook his fist and began to walk away muttering "You will see me soon". He was lost from view when the trees began to shake in an unholy wind. I struggled to my feet shouting "Lottie, Lottie". The whole forest was moving and bending in the storm and I did not see the branch that knocked me unconscious onto the freezing ground.

A Christmas tale. part 4.

"Old Eleanor" was a witch, or so they said. I woke up on a rough stone floor in front of a roaring fire. The drink she gave me was not delicious but it raced through my blood charging my body with a new energy and diminishing the pain in my head where the branch struck. How I got to be there I could not tell.

She was sitting in a rocking chair and she was dressed all in black. The room was full of the gifts of nature. Herbs and leaves hanging from the beams and glass pots on the shelves full of fruit jams and concoctions I could not know. Her hair was grey and long and her face was not beautiful but not the face of a witch. "You have met the Rigbye then?". I told her about our encounter and she looked into the fire. She told me that he had become a wild creature after a bad experience in his childhood. He had been a regular churchgoer until a fateful day when something changed him. Living wild in the woods around the hill he had very little contact with people. "He seems to know you though", she said.

I told her about the old gold coin and the weird things that were either happening or I was imagining. She told me that if the coin is the reason that he knew me then I should be very careful and not come around here at night. "He has become obsessed with the past, he is part of a very old family, what you have found is the key to his troubles".

Then I realised Lottie was lost. "Have you seen my little dog? I must find her". She helped me to her door and I thanked her for her kindness. Her cottage was built out of the sandstone of the hill and covered in moss and lichen. Only the ivy trimmed around the windows revealed it as a house.

"Before you go you must know. Beware Rigbye. If you want to find the answer you must go to Eccleston church. When a promise is broken the pain is for all eternity." The door closed and the black night followed my walk home.

A Christmas tale - part 5.

"It is Elizabethan, around 1600 I would say". The fat jolly priest was sitting in front of his blazing fire in the presbytery. Studying the coin that lay on the rag. On my journey to the church the snow had become increasingly deep and was drifting making the lanes impassable. On the slow journey I had shouted for Lottie but she never came. I was constantly aware of the feeling of being followed by something however.

"You found this in a tree you say?". I explained that it was embedded in a cut log. We both had a glass of sherry in our hands to protect against the winter chill I think. Outside a huge beech tree festooned with snow dominated the garden with its grisly shadows.

The priest picked up the coin. Each light in the room flashed in increased brightness; the fire roared and a great distant voice shouted "Recant!". Every bell in the church and house started to ring. The sherry had been spilt and illuminated through the window of the presbytery was a man hanging from a limb of the beech tree. A softer voice said "No, my lord".

A few moments later all seemed to return to normal. The spectre had vanished. Then the priest told his tale:-

"John Rigby was born in 1570 at Harrock Hall, Eccleston, near Chorley, Lancashire, the fifth son of Nicholas Rigby, by his wife Mary. In 1600 Rigby was working for Sir Edmund Huddleston, whose daughter Mrs. Fortescue was summoned to the Old Bailey for recusancy. Because she was ill, Rigby appeared for her, was compelled to confess his Catholicism, and sent to Newgate. The next day, the feast day of St Valentine, he signed a confession saying that since he had been reconciled to the Roman Catholic faith by Saint John Jones, a Franciscan priest, he had not attended Anglican services. He was sent back to Newgate and later transferred to the White Lion. Twice he was given the chance to recant, but twice refused. His sentence was carried out. He gave the executioner who helped him up to the cart a piece of gold, saying, "Take this in token that I freely forgive thee and others that have been accessory to my death." Rigby was executed by hanging at St Thomas Waterings on 21 June 1600".

This he read from his book and followed it by saying, "The coin you have found is the lost coin of Harrock Hall and was given to the Rigbye family by the executioner. It went missing over 60 years ago". He said the final answer would be found at Harrock Hall itself. I left by the moon as the snow had finally stopped falling.

A Christmas tale - part 6.

The distance from Eccleston church to Harrock Hall is four miles. The drifting snow along the main lanes had made them impassable and only a route through the forest around Harrock Hill was possible. As I entered the the woods the gloom was all around. I lit a lantern that the priest had given me and I continued shouting for Lottie into the darkness.

There was something hanging from a tree branch. It was a small bird, maybe a sparrow, hung by a string. The next was a crow with its throat slit. The next hanging creature was a poor rabbit. Then the next thing I saw! "Oh no not her". There was a fire ahead of me and I walked into the clearing and stood there in the silence. A noose dropped inches from my face and strong arms grabbed me from behind and placed the noose over my head.

The rope became immediately tighter and I was choking and struggling against it but to no avail. Tighter and tighter, it began to lift me off the ground. My feet left the ground and I was hanging. Everything turned black and I stopped breathing.

Then I could see a light at the end of a dark passage in my brain. The light came towards me and a gentle voice whispered in my ear. "No, my lord". The rope became slack and I fell to the wet earth, air flooding my lungs. The fire had been extinguished and I heard a wailing voice disappering into the forest.

When I reached Harrock Hall there were candles burning in the windows and beautiful Christmas decorations adorned the house. It was a magnificent mansion built of Harrock sandstone. The Squire welcomed me, even at this late hour. "Eleanor warned me that you may come, I have been expecting you". I sat down with him in front of the warm fire with a large glass of whisky. That I was most grateful for.

"There is a secret chapel built into the walls of the house. You must come with me to visit it". He pulled aside a tapestry and revealed a thick oak door. We passed through and climbed the stone steps....

A Christmas tale - last part.

At the end of the tight spiral staircase was another locked door. The Squire opened it with an old iron key. Behind the door was the secret chapel. The little altar bare and abandoned by time and disuse. But in the corner a little table with a white cloth and a burning

candle in front of an ancient painting of the martyr. An empty wooden saucer lay on the cloth. I placed the coin in the saucer.

Somewhere in the distance a creature screamed.

Beside the fire again with another glass the Squire told me that before his time the coin had gone missing from the chapel when a group of church children were allowed to visit the hall. Nobody knew who had taken it.

I walked home glad to return the coin and then I saw him in the morning light. Old Rigbye, noose around his neck and preparing for his own death. "Don't blame yourself old man, little sins we may commit as children can rule all our lives, all is well now". I took him down

and a bright pink dawn broke over Pendle to the east. We wandered down the lane together.

Now here is a thing. Chasing mysteries and looking for your dog gives you no time to prepare for the festivities of Christmas. So I knew we were going back to a house with no food and no fire. Walking with a stranger beside me I said "The tattoo?" he told me it is Latin for recant. He had stolen the the coin. He was a child then. His crime never left him.

Unlocking the door I could see a glow coming from the kitchen. Opening the door there resplendant in front of us the table, as before, a magnificent turkey cooked to perfection. The roasted vegetables, sausages, stuffing, flagons of steaming bishop,porter and jugs of wine and all decorated with the beauty of winter. Holly and ivy. Bathed in the candlelight of two brass candelabra.

Lottie was sitting on Old Eleanor's knee, old John Rigbye clutched my arm. My frail, ancient housekeeper Melanie brought him to a chair muttering "No booze for the tramp" and explained that the Squire had sent us a perfect Christmas feast thanking us for the return of the coin. Then she scuttled off to her scullery (whatever that is?) What a time we all had. Lottie had been found by Eleanor. I said to the supposed witch. "How did you find Lottie?", she said "Lottie came to my door carrying something bright and shiny and silver in her teeth, would you like to see it?"......

Merry Christmas. God Bless us Every One. XXX

Printed in Great Britain
by Amazon

79496887R00098